Damage

Damage

Notes on a Queer Aesthetic

Jonathan Alexander

Fordham University Press New York 2026

Fordham University Press also publishes its books in a variety of electronic formats. Some content that appears in print may not be available in electronic books.

Visit us online at www.fordhampress.com.

For EU safety / GPSR concerns: Mare Nostrum Group B.V., Doelen 72, 4831 GR Breda, The Netherlands, gpsr@mare-nostrum.co.uk

Library of Congress Cataloging-in-Publication Data available online at https://catalog.loc.gov.

Printed in the United States of America

28 27 26 5 4 3 2 1

First edition

To be stoic is to become rigid, with Narcissus' beautiful eyes. We took count of all the pain that the executioner could possibly levy upon each inch of our body; then heart wrung, we went and coped.

—René Char, *Leaves of Hypnos*, 4

Contents

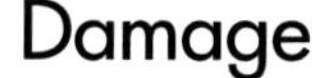

Damage

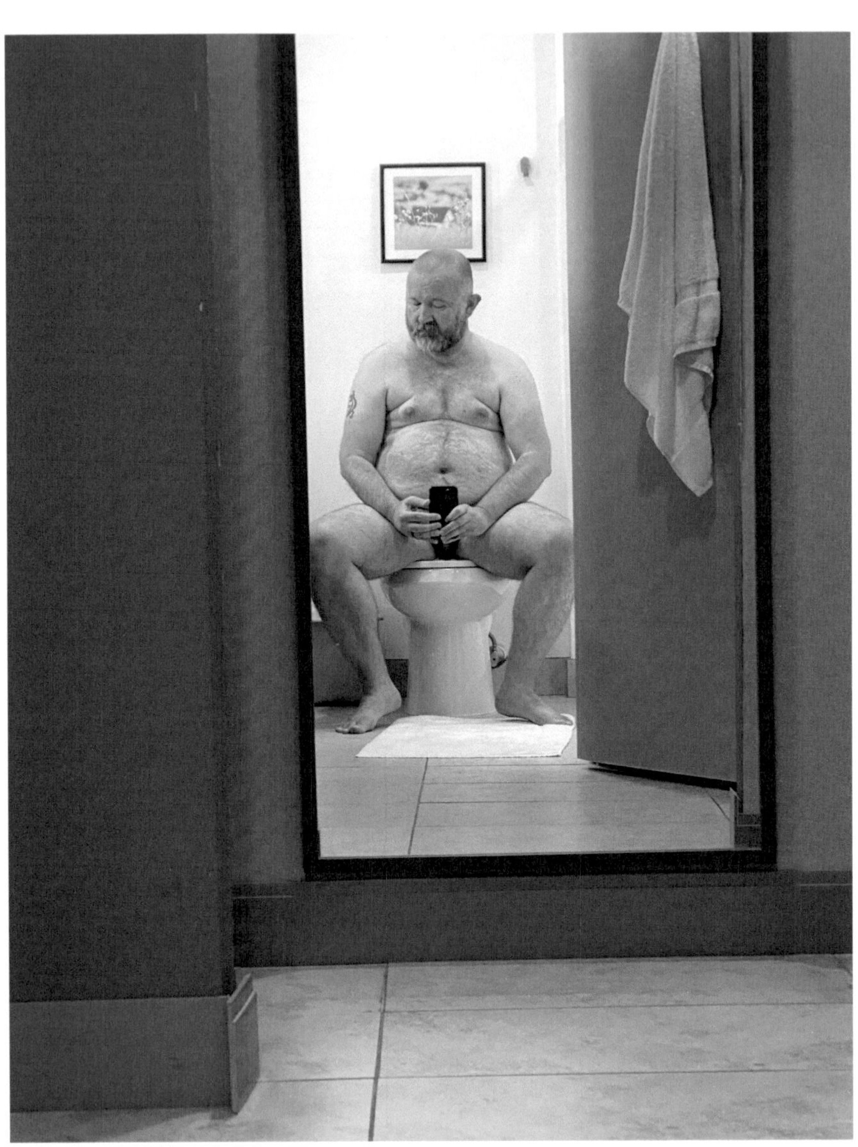

Beginnings

I start with an image of me sitting on the toilet, my obese body bulging in the middle, my naked fleshiness on full display. I write this sentence, starting to describe this image, and I immediately wonder: *Why did I take this picture?* Not *Why am I sharing it with you* now, but more fundamentally, *Why did I even take this picture in the first place?*

To be blunt: The image feels like an act of aggression. It's one of the first things you see when you pick up this book and (quite naturally) turn to the opening pages. A fat, naked, balding man, sitting on a toilet. *Has he no shame? Why accost an innocent reader with such an image?* I wouldn't blame you for asking such questions. I, in fact, anticipate such questions.

I anticipate them because, in another way, the image might not just be an act of aggression against you, a reader, but also against *me*, the one who took the photograph in the first place and then decided to open this book with it. I'm putting my naked and obese body, in a particularly vulnerable moment, on display. How can that *not* be an act of aggression directed at myself? Have I, indeed, no shame?

Or am I *beyond* shame?

I pose this question, and I immediately think that it doesn't make much sense. I am most definitely not beyond shame.

So then, is my offering this photography of my fat, naked, vulnerable body a way to address, perhaps *combat* shame? Or am I *leaning* into it, leaning *into* the shame, in an attempt perhaps to transform it into something else?

So much depends on what you see, right? I cannot know what you see, but what do I see? I need to tell you because an image, even a photographic image seemingly gesturing to the "real," can only tell you so much.

So, again: What do *I* see?

I see me, a fat, balding, white, older man, naked on the toilet. I am queer, though that may not be obvious (though I have been told many times, so many times, throughout my life that my queerness is *so obvious*). My rolls of flesh might suggest some ill health, and that would be correct. I've already had a minor stroke, something called an eye stroke, in which a small globule of cholesterol broke free from the wall of an artery and came to a stopping point in a branch artery of my retina, creating a blind spot and taking some of my vision away. I can no longer drive. I am being treated for hypertension. These things are not visible in the image, but the fatness suggests them—or, at the very least, I cannot look at myself and *not* see those suggestions, those markers of bodily damage, and the underlying damage to which they attest.

And there it is. *Damage*. I am damaged. My body shows it. It's what I dominantly see when I see this image. Moreover, the fact that I take a selfie of my fat and damaged body and print it for others to see speaks to its own kind of damage—something internal, something wrong *inside*, not just physically, not just the globules of cholesterol potentially breaking free and taking bits of my life away, but also something *mental*, something psychological. What kind of person would take such a photo and put it on display unless they were, indeed, damaged?

If you think that, you wouldn't be wrong.

Damaged.

What else is not immediately visible, but that this damaged body might suggest?

I've already said that I am queer. What I didn't say is that I grew up queer in the very late 1960s and '70s in the Deep South, coming into sexual awareness during the height of the AIDS epidemic, believing (as I was told constantly by family, church, school, government) that AIDS was the just and divinely ordained punishment for homosexuals who deserved to burn in the eternal fires of damnation.

This story isn't new. It frankly doesn't even feel all that special any more. It's become a part of history, the tale of a moment in time.

Or is it? Is it just a moment in time? For sure, the specificity and particularity of that moment in time has come and gone. But when I look at the picture of my fat ass sitting on that toilet, I believe that I can see that history. I believe that I am *looking* at that history. I am looking at the leftover damages of those experiences of myself, a young and scared kid, believing that his queerness was going to send him to hell after a loveless and diseased life of anguish and despair. I see in the folds of fat the botched coping mechanisms of eating and drinking that are toxic attempts to numb myself, to feel good about myself, to smother and drown for just a bit the voices of self-hatred given to me when I was a child. I am looking at my damage, and I see that damage both outside *and* inside because I know what I'm looking at, and I know what it's like to live a life now partially blind because I mistreated my body in an attempt to feel better about myself.

I sit on the toilet and look in the mirror. I see the damage. I see myself. I take the photograph.

And then . . .

And then . . . I love myself a little bit.

I do not know how this happens. But taking the photograph, for me, is never just documenting my damage, my self-hatred. It's also a bit like love.

Or something.

No, it's not a reversal or a reclaiming or an act of resistance to consumer culture regimes of body fascism. It's not, now, a declaration of love for my fatness (though I have absolutely no judgment for people who are proudly fat). It's not a recuperation of my self-hatred through an embrace of my bear and daddy phase (though I won't deny the charms of being a bearish daddy). It's not a plea for self-acceptance in a youth-obsessed gay culture that looks right through me (even though I'm a bit relieved at times not to be seen). No. I still feel fat and old and gross. I still feel damaged.

Damaged.

But not *just*. Not only.

Something else.

Looking in the mirror and taking the photograph, making the image and then manipulating it in black and white, accentuating the shadows to highlight the curves . . . This is a something else. This feels like a particular kind of *queer* damage. And a desire to *see* that queer damage. And then to figure out how to love it.

Or something.

This is a book about those images, those moments that capture the meeting point of queer damage and . . . possibility. I hesitate to fill in the second term because it will shift and slide over the course of the images we look at, even as the first term—damage—might seem to remain constant.

This book is *not* about the ubiquity of images and the damage they do. That seems so incredibly banal at this point. In case you hadn't noticed, my phone is with me all the time, its camera seeing far more action than my genitals have in quite a while. Is there anything more banal to say at the beginning of the twenty-first century? That's not even really a question.

With that said, I am tempted to argue that we constantly take pictures because we resent history, we hate ourselves as creatures moving through history, we want to stop our own becoming history, or at least our own aging. We want, generally, to remember ourselves in the good times.

Except for me. I want the image of me not only becoming history but of history hurting me, damaging me, having left its mark.

Like me taking a selfie of what my damage, my vulnerability, looks like, I'm drawn to the images of our pain, our queer pain. This is not always fashionable, I know. Queers have had enough of pain, apparently. But I haven't. Not because I can't get enough of it (or can I?) but because it is never not with me.

(That may be a generational problem. There are moments when I hope it is a generational problem.)

But also because it's so fucking beautiful.

Let's have another example.

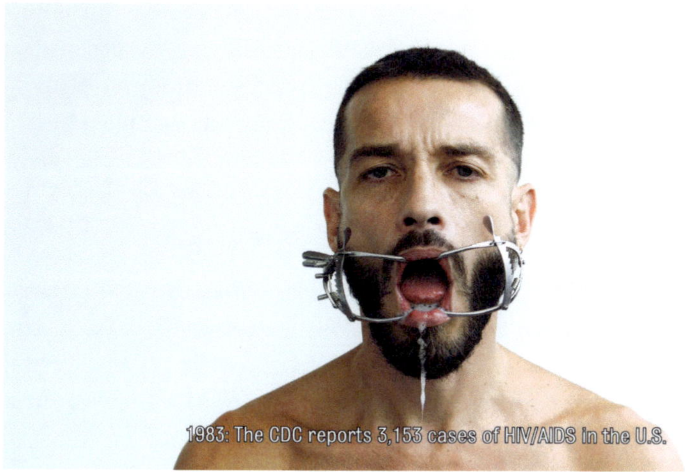

Carlos Motta, *Legacy*, 2019 (still). Courtesy of Carlos Motta; P.P.O.W, New York; Galeria Vermelho, São Paulo; and mor charpentier, Paris and Bogotá.

Here is a screenshot of artist Carlos Motta performing *Legacy*.[1]

Famed New York Gallery P.P.O.W., long a supporter of queer artists and art, continually presented the video from which this image was taken on World AIDS Day, December 1, 2019. Here's how the gallery described *Legacy*:

> Documenting an endurance performance, *Legacy* shows Motta wearing a dental gag while struggling to repeat a timeline of HIV/AIDS history that is clearly articulated off-camera by journalist Ari Shapiro. The onslaught of factual detail begins scientifically, in the early 20th Century, as the virus transfers from animals to humans, as humans begin exhibiting symptoms and transmitting the virus to others, and as medical professionals identify an increasingly urgent crisis.
>
> As the timeline approaches the millennium and AIDS is established as an epidemic, efforts to contain the virus and educate the public are met with increasing moral and legal obstacles, individual stories are unfairly exploited, and the virus becomes medically, culturally, and politically linked to the history of queer liberation.

1 See the full video at https://vimeo.com/351268290.

> Over the course of 30-minutes, Motta becomes visibly exhausted; his speech is more and more labored, and saliva fills his mouth and pours down his chin. The toll of his disrupted breathing and his sheer agony also compromises his short-term memory. As the task of reaching the present becomes physically overwhelming for Motta, we learn that AIDS persists as a global pandemic and, as of 2018, over 37 million people throughout the world are diagnosed.[2]

When I first saw this video, I was stunned—first, by how beautiful Motta is. Perhaps you are too, by how attractive his face is, the intensity of his face, even as it twists in discomfort from the dental gag. Other images and stills from the video capture Motta struggling more and more to articulate the message about AIDS and its ongoing horror. In a way, he only becomes more beautiful the more his words slur, the more pain he seems to suffer.

This is not a BDSM image; the video is not pornographic. The video and related images are not designed to arouse sexually. Are they designed to arouse pity? Some other affect designed to *move* a spectator? What they may be *designed* to do, what they *are* seems unmistakable to me: The video and the stills from it present queer damage, the damage suffered by queer people *because* they are queer, but it is also, just as much, about queer people *taking on that damage and pain* to do something with it.

To do what? Heal it? Transform it? Overcome it? Defy it? Maybe. For some viewers, and artists, maybe some of that, maybe all of that.

Or maybe not.

Like my selfie, Motta's video, a kind of selfie, is of a certain kind of queer damage. Damage and beauty, but damage nonetheless.

This is a book about five artists who work in and with the visual field. It's specifically about images made by artists who, I believe, like Motta, are working over images of damage—and something else, something approaching beauty, for sure, but never quite leaving the damage behind.

---

2 This text no longer appears on Motta's artist page at P.P.O.W.; however, the gallery replicated it in an Instagram post promoting the event: https://www.instagram.com/p/CllvvzoLHFC/.

Hervé Guibert, Mark Morrisroe, Laura Aguilar, Carlos Martiel, Catherine Opie.

Each offers rich visual imagery, captured here in single images or stills that speak to queer damage and pain, sometimes willingly experienced, at other times provocatively displayed. Each image is arresting, profound, beautiful. They are also often simultaneously unique *and* part of more particular projects designed, enacted, and embodied by the artists. Some, like Guibert's and Morrisroe's, are images of pain endured, the artists willingly allowing themselves to be photographed or recorded in moments of pain, psychic and physical, that stem from their experience of a deeply homophobic culture. Others, such as Martiel's and Opie's, are about pain and damage that are self-inflicted—but self-inflicted in the sense that their willingness to take on pain is, in part, a complex synecdoche for larger structures that position queer bodies as permeable and, very often, deserving of pain. And other work, like that of Aguilar, lies somewhere between the two, with her body bearing the traces of the pain of being queer, and specifically queer-of-color, in this culture, while also meditating on self-harm as a way to explore, perhaps even cope with such pain and damage.

Not all of these pains are fungible; they are not equivalent or readily interchangeable. But they are deeply and provocatively connected to the experience of homophobia and queerness in contemporary Western culture.

With that said, this book is *not* about making queer pain beautiful, even if it sometimes is. Rather, it's about using the artwork as a space of meditation on how to survive *with pain*. Note: I did not say *survive pain*. But *with* it. *With* the damage, the damage done.

(I type this out, try to type the word "damage," and it comes out as "image," my computer's subconscious having absorbed, perhaps, my own predispositions, my obsessions, the trace of so much writing about pain and damage and pleasure and possibility.)

More to the point: *I am less interested in transforming pain than in living with it, being in it, and also desiring through it, never not touched by it, for sure, but also not quite determined by it, even if I can never escape it.*

This is also a book about visual images that gesture to the profundity of personal pain *and* queer communion, queer possibility. Images about working on ourselves—*and each other*—through the images shared, circulating, provoking.

Even as I approach these images, and their histories, as objects of meditation, I have to say that this book is not a history, not even really an appreciation.[3] It's a response, an engagement in which I'm not going to hesitate to recognize, even privilege at times, my own embodied reactions. As Francis Bacon famously said about his portraits and self-portraits, I want to catch the moment when the work I am drawn to hits my nervous system, and in turn render that experience as work hitting *your* nervous system.

This book is, inevitably, deeply personal, my archive a chosen one, even if the choosing felt like a compulsion, a propulsion.

As such, it's a *curious* archive, one collected piecemeal over many years. Archives can indeed seem like haphazard assemblages, haphazard until you sit down to reflect on the odds and ends, bits and pieces. A comparison and contrast might help here, especially with another book that looks carefully at an archive of images. Sally Mann's *Hold Still: A Memoir with Photographs* brings together images and texts to tell part of the author's life story in response to family photographs that she finds in boxes of family papers. In approaching the boxes, Mann wonders if she'll find, "in the interest of narrative," a "payload of southern gothic," from "deceit and scandal" to "alcoholism, domestic abuse . . . clandestine affairs . . . blow jobs, suicides, [and] hidden addictions." She finds, she says, "all of it and more."[4] My approach to such life writing here, in my own book, is perhaps less a discovery of damages accumulated over the course of a familial genealogy and more the tracing of queer

3 *An Alternative History of Photography* (New York: Prestel, 2022), by Phillip Prodger, does excellent work in canon busting and the need not just to pay attention to global contributions to the photographic arts but also to recenter the histories of photography with reference to lesser-known artists from around the world.

4 Sally Mann, *Hold Still: A Memoir with Photographs* (New York: Back Bay Books, 2016), xiv.

"family" resonances across networks of relationality—relations built not through blood but through a shared (if ever differentiating) sense of outsiderness.

Maybe this archive will in some way resonate with you. Maybe it will somehow be emblematic of a particular way of thinking about queerness and representation and embodiment and possibility in this particular moment, a moment in the early twenty-first century both of queer emergence *and* disavowal, of queer surges and oppression.

However it may strike, I would be less than honest if I kept from you how my meditations come out of questions I've been asking myself for decades.

What do you do when you already have suffered damage and want to itch it, pick at the scab, not so much to see what's underneath it but to feel something, even if only the shadow of a former, unbearable pain?

Let's put this another way. When your entire culture is pathological, is it not better to live in a pathological relationship to it, picking at your wounds till they seep again?

At the same time, I want to eschew a genealogical approach to my masochism. I've had enough of origins, of roots, even as I recognize the temptation of exploring such, again and again. After all, trauma is imminently narratable. We have little trouble describing the horror. The difficult thing is talking about what comes after. The difficult thing is narrating survival.

The difficult thing is living with the damage already done.

Mine is an archive that, however personal, has obviously not been assembled in a vacuum.

In assembling and reflecting on the work in these pages, on queer damage, some of it self-inflicted, I can't *not* think of Gilles Deleuze's *Coldness and Cruelty*, his extended essay on masochism, in which the philosopher bends over backward to assure us that "the masochistic ego is only apparently crushed by the superego. What insolence and humor, what irrepressible defiance and ultimate triumph lie hidden behind an ego that claims to be so weak."[5] I love Deleuze, at times, but this seems so vitalist, so *recuperative* of the image of damage, so desiring to mitigate the horror, especially of self-inflicted pain. He asserts, *There's something really* good *there, I know it, I promise. There* must *be, something* life-affirming.

It's such a common move, it turns out. Critics refract one another, bending themselves over backwards to maintain the vitality embedded in the embrace of pain. Witness Andy Campbell in *Bound Together: Leather, Sex, Archives, and Contemporary Art*, channeling queer theorist Elizabeth Freeman, whom he quotes to argue that what might "even be intrinsic to the constitution of leather sexualities [is how] 'S/M relentlessly physicalizes the encounter with history and thereby contributes to a reparative criticism that takes up the materials of a traumatic past and remixes them in the interest of new possibilities for being and knowing.'"[6] What do we read here except a kind of doubling, a doubling of pain that is both historicizing and reparative, a past trauma and a new way of being and knowing, so that pain, even pain willfully embraced, is always circulating into new possibilities?

I won't say this is wrong *necessarily*. It's just not *everything*, and maybe only a small part of what happens for me when I look at the images discussed in this book. I prefer instead Cynthia Wu's more ambiguous, ambivalent approach, apparent in the title of her essay: "It Depends: Academic Labor and the Materiality of the Body," in which she writes about the pain of writing itself: "Whether accompanied by pain, pleasure, or both, writing is an act borne on the body." Even more to the point: "I do not want to glamorize the state of being in pain, which Elaine Scarry contends is inarticulable to others and, therefore, isolating. Sometimes (but only sometimes), it is. But neither do I want to relegate it to that of mere deficit or obscure the possibility of finding pleasure in the midst of a life where

5 Gilles Deleuze, *Coldness and Cruelty*, trans. Jason McNeil (New York: Zone Books, 1991), 124.

6 Andy Campbell, *Bound Together: Leather, Sex, Archives, and Contemporary Art* (Manchester: Manchester University Press, 2020), 5.

it exists."[7] Unlike Campbell's doubling of pain through Freeman, Wu bends her thinking around Scarry into a qualification, even a casting of doubt. It's a holding in tension of things, experiences, and intensities that shouldn't always be collapsed into one another, into some "triumph" (to use Deleuze's word) pulled out of trauma.

Oh, I get it. This isn't a fashionable move. I know what people want now. In *Abundance: Sexuality's History*, Anjali Arondekar, announces up front and boldly that "my book challenges . . . an epistemological preoccupation with loss as the structuring mode of narration for histories of [especially queer] sexuality." Almost in defiance of loss, the commitment to abundance continues, constituting a new ethic of queerness: "What historical forms does abundance take when we turn to subaltern peoples and pasts? How do such forms of abundance fall outside historical interest and preservation? How might a turn to abundance work against the imperative to fix sexuality within wider historical structures of vulnerability, damage, and loss?"[8] I read this book, excited, the day I got it in the mail, and the word *damage* here jerked me out of my chair. I felt called out. I know I'm lingering in the damage. But, fuck me, it *is* an imperative, not so much a choice. Oh, I get it: Not everything is loss, loss, loss—but, for some of us, it's never *not* that too.

And I understand, even at times embrace, the politics of a certain kind of recuperation, a working *against* the imperative to "fix" queerness "within wider historical structures" of damage, even a desire for abundance. I've been very moved by the work of Saidiya Hartman, who, in her extraordinary *Wayward Lives, Beautiful Experiments: Intimate Histories of Social Upheaval*, mines the archives for stories of early twentieth-century figures who were living their lives over and against the racist, heteronormative paradigms that otherwise stifled, constricted, pathologized, and criminalized alternative forms of living, loving, and creating family. Early in her book, Hartman relates

---

7 Cynthia Wu, "It Depends: Academic Labor and the Materiality of the Body," in *Sex, Identity, Aesthetics: The Work of Tobin Siebers and Disability Studies*, ed. Jina B. Kim et al. (Ann Arbor: University of Michigan Press, 2021), 41, 43.

8 Anjali Arondekar, *Abundance: Sexuality's History* (Durham, NC: Duke University Press, 2023), 2, 30.

the story of her coming upon an old Thomas Eakins photograph of a nude African American girl, which sparked her imagination to explore the often undocumented, unrecorded, and forgotten lives of those who may have much still to teach us now about living differently. Despite Eakins's exploitative "documentation" of the young Black girl for his own artistic projects, Hartman found something *pressing* in the image: "The how-to-live and *the fierce urgency of the now* can be perceived in these other photographs, the images lost and found, imagined and anticipated, like stills edited from an unfinished movie." Hartman wonders what movie would have been made had such a film even been conceivable: "Was it possible to annotate the image? To make my words into a shield that might protect her, a barricade to deflect the gaze and clock what had been exposed?"[9] I love here the doubleness, the desire to have the images speak, to "annotate" them, but also to protect them, to "shield" the folks lost to time.

But note: She's asking if it's *possible. Can* she protect them, shield them, deflect the damaging gaze, the traumatizing exposure to homophobia, transphobia, racism, classism, to human hatred of difference. She can't. She knows she can't, even if her book is a testament, a testimony, to her wanting to try.

And part of the problem is that she's dealing with images, with leftover images, with ephemeral photography. She wants to save the young Black girl not just from Eakins but from what Eakins represents, from how Eakins himself *represents* the lives of others.

Another question: What if we linger with the image, both damaged and rendering the damage? What if we do both? Linger in the damage *and* note our desire to recuperate it, make it mean something different, something better, something other—but not to eradicate the damage, not even to transform it, but to hold both the pain and the possibility *together*, at the same time, finally, together?[10]

---

9 Saidiya Hartman, *Wayward Lives, Beautiful Experiments: Intimate Histories of Social Upheaval* (New York: W. W. Norton, 2019), 24, 26.

10 Writing about the photographic work of Carrie Mae Weems, bell hooks says that Weems's work is characterized in part by "the will to search out spaces of recovery and renewal." *Art on My Mind: Visual Politics* (New York: New Press, 1995), 71. I'm drawn to that phrasing—"spaces of recover and renewal"—but am

Such questions gesture not just to the conundrums of damage and masochism but also to the complexities and contradictions of the photographed image itself, because any image, no matter how seemingly realistic, is only ever just a representation, a mediation, and thus a distancing from reality. In a way, this distancing allows someone like Hartman to read into the photograph of a young Black girl all of the possibilities otherwise elided by its production in Eakins's studio; Eakins takes the photograph, but he can't determine how it will ultimately be "read" by others.[11]

Indeed, Roland Barthes makes the profoundly personal way we encounter photographs one of their prime virtues. Barthes's major theoretical contribution to the interpretation of photography lies in the *punctum*, that oh so personal pricking or puncturing that a photograph effects on an individual, a nontransferable wound, a cut, deeply felt—so deeply felt and so personal that Barthes won't show us the picture of his mother that pierces him. We wouldn't get it, he maintains, so he keeps it to himself. (A whiff of the closet here, no? Wanting to keep the secret response a secret just a little bit longer?)[12]

But this distancing is also a potential problem, especially in an increasingly image-saturated culture in which images, densely circulating, can come to seem more real than reality, the representations

---

mindful that such a space is never found, or even approached, without a *search* and a *will*. What happens if we suspend the search, let the will rest for a moment and dwell in the antechamber to any space of recovery and renewal? That's what I think I'm doing in this book.

11 I want to make clear that I have little interest in the conversation about whether photographs, or photographs of visually rich works of performance, are works of art. They are in the world and are available for engagement, indeed *invite* engagement, and I intend in this book to engage them as they evoke and provoke in me opportunities to think queerly about systemic forms of violence. If you're interested in the question of photography as art, you could not do much better than start with Michael Fried's *Why Photography Matters As Art As Never Before* (New Haven, CT: Yale University Press, 2008).

12 See *At the Edge of Sight: Photography and the Unseen* (Durham, NC: Duke University Press, 2013) for Shawn Michelle Smith's critique of Barthes's racism in *Camera Lucida*. Another book that may be of similar interest is Carol Mavor's *Black and Blue: The Bruising Passion of Camera Lucida, La Jete, Sans soleil, and Hiroshima mon amour* (Durham, NC: Duke University Press, 2012).

conditioning and shaping how we understand what is real. At the end of *Camera Lucida*, this book that is almost a memoir (almost), Barthes frets about how we now seem to "live according to a generalized image-repertoire."[13] Surrounded by them, images seem to replicate into our lives, shaping our perceptions, our phenomenological apprehension of the world around us. The "queerness" of this lies in part in how he's updating Oscar Wilde, who had written in "The Decay of Lying" that many Londoners at the end of the nineteenth century didn't see evening dusk anymore, but rather James McNeill Whistler's *representation* of evening dusk, the painter's work having conditioned people's perception. In sum: *Life imitates Art far more than Art imitates Life.*[14] Barthes expands this notion, silently, not alluding to Wilde, but if you know, you know that he's pulling at the threads on an old queen's idea.

And then, and *then*, in the final pages, the last two pages, Barthes offers an example of this very queer idea—that we don't see anything "naturally" anymore, and that our sight is conditioned by artificial and mediated images—by going into a New York porn shop, an "extreme example," and talking about seeing images in which, Jane Gallop writes, "it is as if the anonymous individual (never an actor) who gets himself tied up and beaten conceives of his pleasure only if this pleasure joins the stereotyped (worn-out) image of the sadomasochist: pleasure passes through the image: here is the great mutation." The great mutation! The great mutation? It is what it sounds like. Barthes, after teasing us for so many pages with an image that pierces him to the soul and that he'll never show us, now suggests that the circulation of BDSM porn images actually interferes with our capacity to experience the pleasures of erotic pain because we're more focused on the image than on the bodily sensations. He calls this problem not just a mutation but a "reversal," in the sense that it replaces an intensity of direct experience with the reproduction of an image. Or, as he puts it, "Such a reversal necessarily raises the ethical question:

---

13 Roland Barthes, *Camera Lucida*, trans. Richard Howard (New York: Hill & Wang, 2010), 118.

14 See Oscar Wilde, *The Decay of Lying: And Other Essays* (New York: Penguin Books, 2010).

not that the image is immoral, irreligious, or diabolic (as some have declared it, upon the advent of the Photograph), but because, when generalized, it completely de-realizes the human world of conflicts and desires, under cover of illustrating it."[15]

There's more here than just Barthes tipping his hand a bit as a gay man, a gay writer, showing us his knickers, as it were—though there's plenty of that too. There's the profoundly disturbing thought that images, even of a particular queer kind of "sexual perversion," might "de-realize" our world, invite us to experience less the "world of conflicts and desires," as opposed to the realness of the experience of those conflicts and desires. Photographs, even of the most intimate kind, might distance us not just from each other but from ourselves, from our very capacity to experience—even when what we desire is the experience of pain itself.

Susan Sontag worries over a similar problem in *Regarding the Pain of Others*, in which she expresses concern over the rapid and increasing circulation of images of pain, atrocity, violence, and harm. She writes, "One can feel obliged to look at photographs that record great cruelties and crimes. One should feel obliged to think about what it means to look at them, about the capacity actually to assimilate what they show."[16] Indeed, what *do* such images mean? Sontag worries that images inviting us to regard the pain of others might, as Barthes suggest, produce more *distance* than immediacy, more potential aloofness than actual *regard*.

Sontag attempts to address the concern of distancing this way: "It is felt that there is something morally wrong with the abstract of reality offered by photography; that one has no right to experience

---

15 Jane Gallop, "The Pleasure of the Phototext," in *Photography Degree Zero* (Cambridge, MA: MIT Press, 2009), 118. See that book for more on Barthes's differentiation between pornography and erotica: "For Barthes, pornography is pure *studium* whereas the erotic occurs when there is a *punctum*. . . . For Barthes, pornography is a self-enclosed image: it is sexuality contained, sexuality that does not leave its frame. The viewer can worship it in a kind of masturbatory way but can neither touch it nor be touched by it" (51).

16 Susan Sontag, *Regarding the Pain of Others* (New York: Farrar, Straus and Giroux. 2003), 95.

the suffering of others at a distance, denuded of its raw power; that we pay too high a human (or moral) price for those hitherto admired qualities of vision—the standing back from the aggressiveness of the world which frees us for observation and for elective attention. But this is only to describe the function of the mind itself."[17] Sontag turns a necessity into a virtue here. We are, after all, *always* at a distance from each other. The photograph of someone else's pain is, in a way, just a reminder that we are already at a remove from that person's experience of pain. It is not the immediacy that is important for Sontag, but rather the invitation to *regard the pain*.[18] And one can only regard it as a form of reflection, or meditation.

Now, take this insight a step further. What if we are invited to regard images that are not just about suffering, violence, atrocity—but are

17 Ibid., 118. For further discussion on Sontag and her approach to metaphor and metaphorical thinking, see Jay Prosser, "Metaphors Kill: 'Against Interpretation' and the Illness Books," in *The Scandal of Susan Sontag*, ed. Barbara Ching et al. (New York: Columbia University Press, 2009). Prosser usefully proposes thinking beyond the metaphors of suffering, as deployed in in *Illness as Metaphor* and *AIDS and Its Metaphors,* and instead trying to get at the truth, or at least think differently, about pain. As Prosser asks, "Can we be ill *outside* of language and metaphors, the functions of narration and interpretation—which might also be ameliorative and help us make sense of suffering?" (200, emphasis added). The question remains an open one for me.

18 Robert Hariman and John Louis Lucaites argue in *The Public Image: Photography and Civic Spectatorship* (Chicago: University of Chicago Press, 2016), with reference to Sontag, that "photography can provide works of the imagination, but they risk being merely fanciful confections. It can bring viewers to see anew or to enjoy a habitual blindness. Sontag was half right: fancy is a risk whenever the imagination is in play. But what she missed is this: the imagination is necessary for reality to be apprehended at all. If only fantasy is possible, then a better way of seeing reality is no more accessible than it was by means of those pellets of information, facts incapable of carrying with them the ideas and emotions needed for thought and action. Stated otherwise, a photograph is always both image and optic: a picture of some part of reality and a way of seeing that reality more extensively; a recording of specific facts and an act of imagining a world" (72). Such reflections prompt me to ask questions: What worlds do we see? What worlds do we imagine? And how can the world pictured in photography helps us imagine a world not just beyond but *through* our damages?

about people, this time queer people, actively foregrounding, even showcasing their suffering, even in some cases *self-inflicted* pain and damage? I'm not talking about the kinds of BDSM images that Barthes ogled in the New York porn shop. I'm talking about images staged as active invitations to regard or meditate upon *queer damage*.

I'm talking about Carlos Motta trying to tell us about AIDS as an ongoing problem with his mouth held willingly open by a metal gag, drool spilling down his bearded chin as his beautiful eyes squint in pain.

I'm talking about my own taking of a selfie of my fat, pasty white, bald ass sitting on a toilet and giving it to you, inviting you to see my body framed in the photograph, an object worthy of your regard.

Such images, and all the images discussed in this book, constitute, at the very least, a *reversal* of how images of queers, damaged queers have been used in the past. I'm thinking of Margo Canaday's *The Straight State: Sexuality and Citizenship in Twentieth-Century America*, in which the historian documents how homosexuals in the midcentury United States, caught by the police loving or pleasuring one another, often had their pictures published in newspapers as examples of deviant criminals, their lives then ruined, their images marking them as outcast perverts, fully damaged goods.[19] Just decades later, the possibility of queers recording their own damage seems at the very least a defiant act, showcasing, in some cases, their pathology, but also just as much foregrounding what a homophobic and transphobic culture does *to* them. Defiance, yes. Defiant while damaged, still.

Defiant, but damaged, still.

Let me put this another way: I want this book to be *in regard—queerly*. I take up the invitation not just to witness but to hold in my hand the images of queer damage, recognizing my distance, while also feeling my connection to these other gay and lesbian and queer people. That connection, I believe, is not just about empathy or

19 Margo Canaday, *The Straight State: Sexuality and Citizenship in Twentieth-Century America* (Princeton, NJ: Princeton University Press, 2009).

even sympathy. It is an invitation, even if I am projecting that invitation onto the images, to experience something different, something unique, even something immediate however distant, about damage, about homophobic damage, about persistence through a variety of kinds of damage.

It is holding in your hand, in your eyes, in your ears, in your mind, in whatever sense you are capable—it is holding damage and possibility together.

Together, at the same time.

Even if you don't know what to do with them, even if you can't make sense of them, even if they never resolve into one another.

Even if, never.

Even if the images, those damaged images, won't go away. Even if the damage, never, goes away.

Let's start years ago, in my late twenties, fresh off a divorce, newly openly queer, if not *newly* queer—for when have I ever not been queer, even when het-married, even when trying and consistently failing to hide my queerness, to the point where I'm never, even now, not sure that I could hide it, marked, visible, Cain-like in my recognized otherness?

I was friends with a slightly older couple, a man and a woman, the man a therapist of the alternative kind, one who practiced past-life regression therapies. After a few nights of hanging out together, he offered me a free session. I went to his house one summer afternoon and lay down on his couch in his home office while he sat, like a psychoanalyst, behind me and to my left. He asked if he could record the session for me, as I might find it interesting to listen to it in the future. Sure, I said, and then he asked me to close my eyes.

How he got me "under," I don't exactly recall, which is probably a testament to his abilities. He was a lovely guy, large, bearlike, daddybear, grizzly but only in the very best and friendliest ways. KT was his name. I remember his wife telling me about him before I met him myself, telling me that she was totally cool with me being queer because she herself had a husband with a girl's name. I never thought of KT as a girl's name, though I get was she was trying to do.

So before I know it, I'm "under." Prepositions are the worst because, as soon as I'm "under," I feel more "up" than anything else, moving, moving very fast, like I'm in flight but not through space, through time. I'm flashing back and forth, into the past, bam bam bam, one shot of my life after another, and then into the future, bam bam bam, one scene after another, flying past, but not so much the scenes flying as me flying, flying through time. At the same time, though, I'm not actually seeing me, as this is not the past and future of my life, but the past and future of all of my lives, past mes and future mes. In a further twist, I'm flying not past their lives, the past and future mes' lives, but past and through all of the moments in which the past and future mes are dying. I'm experiencing all of my past lives and my future lives at their moments of their death.

I hear KT talking to me, leading me through this. (I don't recall now what he said, but I know he was talking to me throughout the session.) He, however, has no idea what I'm experiencing because I remain completely silent through the session. Not one word. I do not speak one word. But his voice continues on, not quite a drone, but a line, a through line, maybe a panic clip that I can hold on to, but I'm otherwise in, totally in, up, under, out there, seeing my past lives, flying toward my future lives, all at the point of those individual lives letting go.

Ok, nothing more metaphorical here than I was recently divorced, a very concrete past life dying, dead, one I was letting go, one that had already let go of me. But also, coming out as queer itself as a kind of dying. Let's not kid ourselves. Even if you're as obviously queer as I was, the moment you publicly embrace that queerness you die, part of you dies, a version of you dies, and a version of you, someone else's version of you, your own version of you you were trying to hold on to—all of these yous die too, and they keep on dying, so many fucking times, they keep on dying. You have to let go, keep on letting go, keep disappointing others that you will not be what they want you to be, what they need you to be in order to sleep a little more soundly at night in their understanding of not just you, but of the world, of themselves. You keep dying, inviting them to die too. And they hate you for it. I'm not surprised at all that my first past-life regression images are saturated with death, past and future. Curiously, though, as I was experiencing all of these lives and deaths, none of it was frightening.

More . . . interesting. Especially the one of me, future me, unknown me, on a spaceship, giving up the ghost as I (or him or us) hurtle past an alien sun.

Then things change. Back on the couch, I'm in a forest, or a wooded area, pine trees all around me, somewhere in southern Louisiana. Who am I kidding? I know exactly where. Outside my aunt and uncle's house in Slidell, Louisiana, a little bedroom community about an hour east of New Orleans. My father's sister and her husband. We'd go there fairly frequently as kids. I'm maybe six or seven. Wandering in the backyard. Feels like fall, chilly but not cold. Stepping on pine cones, my little legs tripping a bit. And then something . . . something bad. A dark gray patch. Something . . . evil is the word. I look around, but I don't remember seeing anyone around me. "Remember" is the wrong word. I "remember" this place, but I don't think this is a memory, or at least I'm not sure. It's more like a scene than a memory. A scene. Something is happening here. Something happened here. But not a memory.

And then . . . something really awful. I am aware that I'm not talking to KT even as I can hear him go on, go on, talking, holding out a line. But I'm not saying a word. Not now, especially not now. I feel my lips pressing further closed, clamping down, making sure I don't talk about what I'm seeing, because what I'm seeing is me as a Nazi doctor, performing the most awful atrocities. I cannot describe them. I won't describe them. I can write that I felt myself, my past life, as a Nazi doctor, but I will not talk about what I did, what I did in those camps.

And then I'm done. KT brings me out of the hypnosis or whatever it was. I'm no longer under, but I don't move. I'm not sure I can move. I just lie there, not moving. That's all I can do, I say to myself in the moment, I'm not moving, I can't move, I don't want to move. I don't know what to do.

Eventually, though, I do move, and KT is gentle with me. I sit up and drink some water, and we talk about what I experienced. I tell him all about the past and future mes dying, and then about the woods outside my father's sister's house, and then, and then, the Nazi doctor. I tell him I am the Nazi doctor. He is, thankfully, skeptical. He says it's possible, but not inevitable. He even says that my queerness in this life might be a karmic way of engendering empathy for other beings, an empathy that I had obviously neglected or suppressed or never really had in my past life as a Nazi doctor. I remember being grateful that he doesn't call my queerness a punishment.

It feels like a punishment at times. It feels like damage. It certainly feels like the least of which I deserve if I had, indeed, been a Nazi doctor.

But the bit in Slidell, in the pine tree forest, that's important, he says. It's important that I saw that, something from my current life, something from this incarnation, before the Nazi doctor entered the scene. He says, sometimes, spirits of the dead wander, often far from where they died, seeking to get away from either their death or the lives they led. They wander, fretting over their lives, their deaths, worried, troubled, trying to get away, looking for something, for release, for innocence. I could have encountered just such a spirit, perhaps the wandering spirit of a long-dead Nazi doctor, and that spirit, seeing me, attached itself to me, wanting my innocence as a child, wanting to comfort itself with my innocence. Perhaps I'd seen a dead animal in that forest, and that experience, the sight of a dead animal, something slightly traumatic like that to a six- or seven-year-old, might have been a psychic blow hard enough to open up my spirit just a little bit, just enough to let in this wandering spirit of a dead Nazi doctor. And that spirit has been with me, confusing his pain for mine, me confusing my pain for his. Seeing him, maybe, just maybe, I was also letting him go, inviting him out of myself, sending him back on his way.

That's a lot of hoop-jumping to convince myself that I wasn't a horrific monster in a past life, I tell KT. Stranger shit happens, he responds. And I hope he's right. I hope I wasn't a Nazi doctor in a past life. I hope that the Nazi doctor is just a strange projection of all the atrocities suffered by queer people at the hands of bigots and fascists and the intolerant. I hope that my psyche is just telling me a complicated tale of how I have internalized some of those atrocities, some of those awful things that people say about queer people, some of the ways that our culture has pathologized queer people, some of the awful things that people do to queer people—and I'm just at times confusing that awfulness with myself.

But however I understand those visions, a story my subconscious was telling about itself, its origins, its futures, its present possibilities, there's nothing but damage all around. Moments of death. A psychic wound. An historical trauma. Nothing by damage, damage everywhere.

The one problem. I have a sound recording of the session, an old audio tape, buried in a box in a garage. But no images to share. No pictures I could bring back with me from this psychic jaunt. Nothing but narrated damage.

But a story nonetheless, and (hopefully) a well-crafted story, so something, if not beautiful, at least somewhat pleasing in the telling and hearing.

But you came here for images, didn't you? So let's have one, one from another haunted soul, one whose own death he himself would describe again and again, anticipating it, narrating it, staging it. Let's have an image of him still young, long before that death, just coming into his own awareness of the many hauntings of a life.[20]

After the story I just told, I can't help but think that Hervé Guibert's cock is a beautiful thing to see.

But the image is also so *vulnerable*. Is there timidity here? Something wrong? The body, the face, the cock are at a distance. Is he scared? Is he wondering why he's taking this picture? He's so . . . *exposed*. But willingly so. Still . . . *exposed*, like me on KT's couch, even if only exposed, at first, inside my head, to myself. More like me on the toilet in the first image in this book, naked and vulnerable.

Then I look closer. I see a shadow in Hervé Guibert's cock, always a shadow.

I need to tell you something now. I need to tell you how this man, this man I never met, is a shadow in my shadow.

20 Christine Guibert, the author's wife, granted permission to reproduce this autoportrait provided that I use the caption, "I'm not queer, just gay." Note that I do not refer to Guibert himself as queer and honor her understanding of his preference for the term "gay" to describe himself—a preference that would have been in keeping with the times in which Guibert lived and wrote.

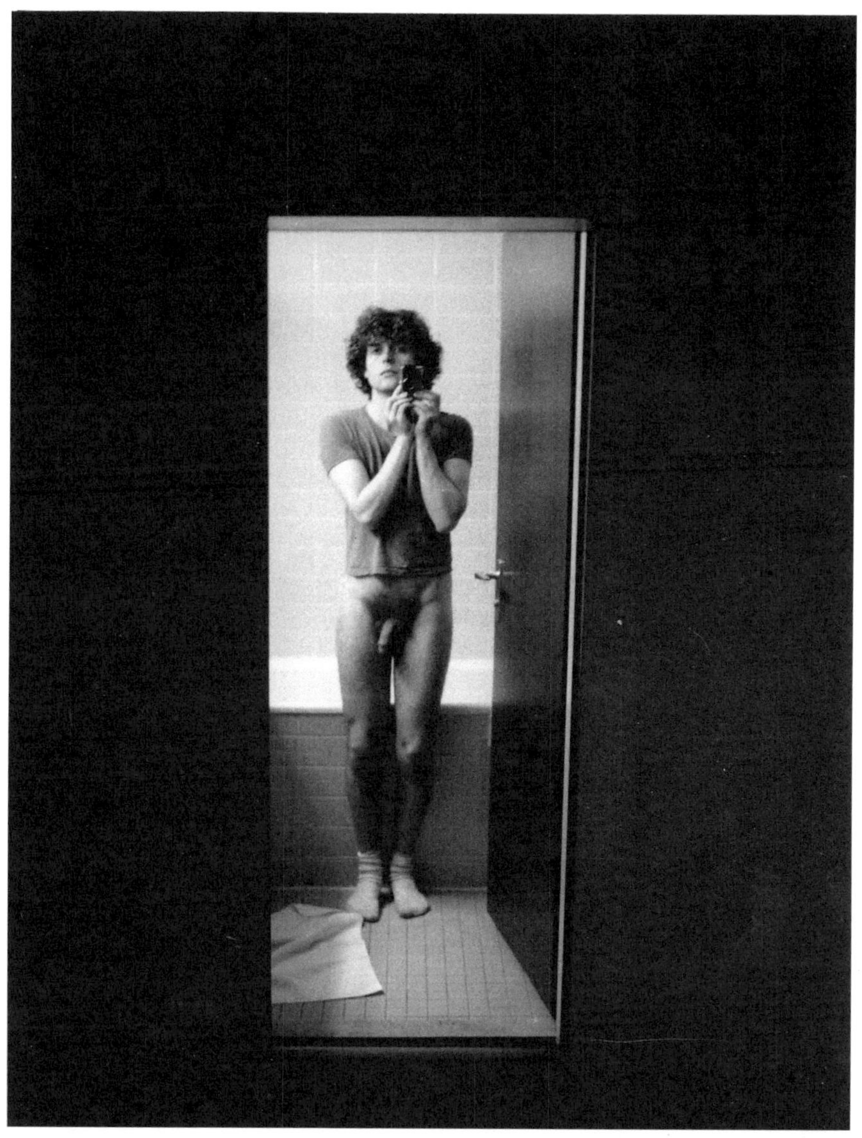

Hervé Guibert, *Autoportrait*: "I'm not queer, just gay." Courtesy of Christine Guibert.

Hervé Guibert

So much to say about Guibert. I'm not sure I'll ever stop writing about him. I can't *not*, not at this point. I wrote things before I discovered Guibert, surely, but nothing I've written after reading him isn't Guibert, Guibert proximate, or Guibert adjacent. He is a shadow in my shadow. He wrote practically nonstop his entire life, and I identify my own writing (writing without wanting it to end) with reading Guibert, obsessively, returning to his books, reading slowly to elongate the experience, not wanting it to end, knowing it won't end because I'll keep going back and then filling in the interstices with my own writing, writing about Guibert, with Guibert, proximate and adjacent to Guibert.

But he also took pictures, just as obsessively it seems, constantly photographing friends, lovers, places, allowing himself to be photographed by friends and lovers, constantly, ceaselessly, even at the end of his life making a movie about the end of his life, writing, writing, photographing, writing, making a movie.

I try to imitate Guibert because I don't want a world without him, even if I am only a shadow's shadow of what he was, of what he could have been if he survived.

A shadow? You are wondering why I think this picture of Guibert showing us himself in a mirror is a picture of damage. Let me be blunt. Photographing one's cock takes a particular form of self-hatred. You set yourself up for the most vicious forms of critique, first from yourself and then from others if you make the picture public.

What is *that? Are you really showing us your* cock*? Is that* all *you've got?*

In Guibert's case, I'm willing to forgive a lot. Objectively, I suppose, there's not much to forgive. He's got a good-looking cock. And he wasn't shy about photographing it, or himself.

Indeed, Guibert took a lot of photos of himself, these autoportraits—which, we must admit, is a word that sounds so much better than "selfie," so much more sophisticated. So *French*. Nonetheless, engaging in making autoportraits, whatever you call them, raises the question of *why*. Why photograph oneself? The contemporary penchant for selfies speaks to a kind of narcissism that wants to stage the self in the best possible life, circulating these narcissistic images through social media as a form of cultural and material capital. Look where I am! Behold how glorious my life is!

The same charge of narcissism seems anachronistic when levied at Guibert. Photographing himself, and his lovers, in the 1980s has a completely different historical valence. Given the homophobia of the time, not to mention the AIDS-phobia, such photographs are complex acts of *self-love*. They are declarations of beauty, of not just acknowledging but *asserting* one's beauty when much of the rest of the world was intent on derogating, actively *erasing*, their existence. To see Guibert's autoportraits as just selfies, even early forms of selfies, is to view them without a historical consciousness, to engage in the erasure of the press of history on bodies and minds and spirits.

In this critical context, my love of Guibert's cock photo is the love that we gays and queers have fought to have for ourselves despite the hatred spewed at us, despite the damages accrued. If I opened this section by saying that "photographing one's cock takes a particular form of self-hatred," I maintain that that statement as just as true as saying that such photographs are a form of self-love—because to assert one's self-love in a homophobic context, one actively lethal to queers, is to nonetheless, despite the odds, take a chance that one's love will overcome the hatred, that one will survive the hatred that one is practically calling on oneself by making such images, much less by putting them into circulation. We are worthy of that chance. We are worthy of that love.

We don't always believe it.

To this day, I am not sure I believe it. I am not sure I am worthy of love.

I have, of course, never seen Hervé Guibert's cock in real life. He died many years ago, in 1991, at the height of the AIDS epidemic in the Western world. I was probably twenty-two, twenty-three, and while I had seen cocks not my own by that point, and while I had even had another boy's cock in my mouth by then, my experience was limited. I have since seen many cocks. Few have propelled me toward activity with them. Few have even simply held my attention. But Guibert's cock? Guibert's cock has my full attention.

With that said, I admit now that I am a particular kind of queer man. I do not adore penises. I do not worship at phallic altars. In fact, I will go so far as to say that I think genitalia are rather unattractive. I worry over whether this is a form of self-hatred, a kind of damage. At the very least it seems a form of *sex*-hatred, a real discomfort with sex. But perhaps it is also just a preference. After all, I adore a good-looking male butt. I'm constantly checking out guys' rears. But their penises are frankly of less interest. Not *no* interest, mind you. I have seen good-looking cocks. But I am not *drawn* to them like I am to a man's ass.

But Hervé Guibert's cock is an exception. It is beautiful. Guibert took a few different pictures of it, but I'm thinking in particular of one photograph, the one I showed you, in which he stands in front of a mirror, without pants but charmingly wearing socks, holding a camera about chest height and snapping a photograph of his member. His tousled hair frames a face only slightly lost in the concentration of getting the shot right. The penis, of quite respectable length, flaccid, is cut and points down, obscuring a view of his balls, surrounded by what might be trimmed pubic hair. A black and white photo, but gradations of gray outline the shadows of his organ.

I won't say I can't take my eyes off this cock, but I have clearly studied it. I declare it to myself an object worthy of study.

I have been thinking about this one particular picture of Guibert's cock because there has been renewed interest in the Frenchman's writing and photography, with more of his voluminous body of work being translated into English and with a recent exhibition of his photographs in France, particularly one at Les Douches la Galerie that marks the thirtieth anniversary of the artist's death.[1] You can easily find online a wealth of past exhibitions with an equal wealth of images, including many "autoportraits," including a few of Guibert's member. Today we would call such an autoportrait not just a "selfie" but a "dick pic."

I have received dick pics. I have also taken nude and partially nude selfies, but I have rarely taken a selfie of my own cock. I can't quite do it. I can't quite overcome my own shame.

Questions emerge. Why would one photograph one's member, and then why would one send such photographs to other people? Some answers are perhaps obvious. Any dick pic I have received has been an attempt to excite me, to arouse my interest. Such attempts to do not really work on me. I even find them somewhat distasteful. This is not what I'm into. And this is perhaps why I do not take many pictures of my own penis. I do not intend to send them anywhere. I do not imagine a teleology of phallic selfies for myself, though I do not judge those who indulge such an imaginary. (An ass pic might be a different story.)

Which brings me back to Guibert's cock. He took this picture not with a cell phone but with a camera, and the film on which this image was imprinted had to be developed. This was not an image made for instant gratification. But was it made then to circulate after development? Could, and did, Guibert upload this image in some form onto the pre-Web internet? I think it highly unlikely, but I can imagine friends and lovers getting a gander of the image. I am not phallically insensate enough to fail to imagine it causing some arousal

1 See https://www.lesdoucheslagalerie.com/en/exhibitions/123-herve-guibert-self-image/ for more information on this exhibition, which ran from November 5, 2021–February 12, 2022.

among the Frenchman's acquaintances. (Did Michel Foucault see this image? Did it arouse the philosopher?)[2]

My parenthetical questions are attempts at self-deflection. Am *I* aroused by this photograph of Guibert's cock? I am going to say *no*. And by that "no" I mean that I have not masturbated to this image. I have not shown it to others and invited them to wonder with me at it as an object of *erotic* interest. You will likely not believe that my interest in this image of Guibert's cock is more, shall we say, *aesthetic* than erotic. But, in my defense, I think that I would find Guibert's loose T-shirt and tube socks more erotically interesting than the flaccid but still rather impressive member. It's the boyishness of the picture that is fetching, charming, sensual, gesturing toward the erotic.

Perhaps, too, what we (and by "we" I mean "I") might read into this image, a reading of a possible reason for its existence, is this: The young photographer is interested, even captivated in his own body, his wonder at himself, and then too perhaps his desire to titillate, him imagining who will see this photograph. T? Vincent? Michel? Roland, even? So many possibilities stem from one image.

I do not know what Guibert was thinking when he took this picture. But I can imagine that taking it might have been exciting, even daring, defiant—hence perhaps the timidity I detect in the face, even some of the distancing through the framing. Defiant, but a little bit *unsure*.

To be sure, we see no physical arousal, but I wonder if there was a small, clear drip of pre-cum when Guibert put his camera down. Did he feel a tingling in his hips, a stirring, as we say, in the groin? Was he a bit turned on by the defiance, even perhaps a bit of the shame of exposing oneself, the shame our culture has done such a good job of installing in gay and queer subjects? Shame can be exciting too,

---

2 Guibert famously wrote about Foucault's death from AIDS while Guibert himself was struggling with HIV disease in *To the Friend Who Did Not Save My Life*, trans. Linda Coverdale (New York: Atheneum, 1991) a roman à clef in which Foucault is represented through the character Muzil, a complex reference to Austrian writer Robert Musil.

especially if you are coming up against it, probing it with your fingers, fingering the wound of the damage of shame inflicted on you.[3]

Such excitation, if not explicit sexual arousal, is embedded in historical and political realities that Guibert spent much of his short life calling attention to, battling, struggling with, refuting, and fucking over—before they eventually fucked *him* over. But we'll get to that in a moment.

Perhaps I am not being completely honest here about my fascination (or expressed lack thereof) with cocks. It's hard to be honest about such things. We do not make it easy for each other to be honest, much less explicit, about such things. And my own queer damage makes me constantly want to deflect attention from what I desire, lest I be found out, exposed.

So, in the interest of honesty, in the interest of exposing myself along the lines perhaps that Guibert has exposed himself in his autoportrait, I admit some fascination with excessive cumming, with the "large load," with fully erect cocks straining to spew forth geysers of semen, lacing a boy's body with sticky thick strings of spooge, the cock throbbing to release yet more and more cum, then an aftershot of jism as the cock quivers one last time. But wait, another throb, an aftershock, the boy's head rolling back, panting with the effort, the mess made. I download one video after another of such cocks spewing forth, the bigger the load the better. Is it the cock I'm interested in? Or its performance? Its capacity to produce so much seed, seed that will lie fallow on the boy's stomach, his chest, his legs, his face, only to be wiped away with a paper towel, washed down a drain? It is the exertion of such effort in the pure pursuit of pleasure that seems so . . . *right*.

3 In *Love and Degradation: Excessive Desires in Queer-Feminist Art* (University Park: Penn State University Press, 2024), William J. Simmons uses the work of Lana Del Rey, Felix González-Torres, and Glenn Ligon, among others, to argue for how "mitigating shame around what motivates our desire for knowledge and feeling is a queer, feminist, and anti-racist project because it works to unseat what we think of as knowledge generally, which has always been the project of progressive scholars" (4).

And then afterward the letdown, the inevitable anticlimax. Even a bit of *shame*. What a waste, perhaps. Why do we begrudge ourselves such pleasure, such solitary delight, in the aftermath of the climax?

Ok, by this point, I'm projecting. I don't know what these boys are thinking. They may not be thinking of or feeling shame at all. And to be fair, after I once shot a load *over my shoulder* I felt no shame, but instead some actual *pride*. Yes, I was proud. I'm bragging even now. I remember sitting in my chair at my desk at home, the desk where I wrote my books, graded my students' papers, corresponded through email with my colleagues and collaborators. I paused in my work to jack off and must have been particularly aroused that day because, my pants slightly lowered, my head lolling back, I jerked and jerked until my cock exploded in a string of cum whose upper reaches landed on the back of my chair over my left shoulder. The *left shoulder* seems an important detail, if only to me. I felt no shame in that moment, or after. Rather, wonder—I felt *wonder*. This is not a daily occurrence. For me, this is a *rare* occurrence, and at my age it's likely never to happen again.

If you haven't grown up with self-hatred, with a queer self-loathing of your queer self, then I'm not entirely sure you can understand the wonder I am talking about. To experience one's body make such pleasure . . . Already I have to stop because I realize how my language betrays me, how when I talk about this pleasure I slip into abstractions: "to experience one's body." Whose body is that if not *my body*? So why do I say "one" and not "my"? *My* body? Our—shit, no, *my* self-hatred manifests at the level of the language I default to in talking about myself.

Photographing oneself and delighting in the excesses of one's—of *our*—bodies seems, in this context, a political act. I have a hard time believing that I am overstating that. It *feels* political. David Halperin has suggested that there is no orgasm without ideology, by which he means that the pleasures we take are so often, if not indeed always, shaped by the social and cultural scripts that normalize and license desire, so that, even if you are engaging in nonnormative erotic practices you are still in a sociocultural and hence broadly political relation. Your desires are political.[4] So, photographing our cocks, and delighting in the spewing of cocks, can be, for queer people in a homophobic political context, a political act. I don't feel this is all that controversial.

The political context is even thicker than overcoming simple internalized homophobia, although there's nothing simple about that, let me tell you.

I cannot look at Guibert's cock in this picture and not think of AIDS. I'm not sure I can look at *any* cock and not think of AIDS, at some level, however backgrounded or distant from overt consciousness. I turned eighteen in 1985, watching Rock Hudson die on national television. I will never not be aware of AIDS, of the possibility of transmission of HIV through a cock.

The erect phallus stands at attention to death.

Overstated? Not if you lived through it. Not if your coming into awareness of your interest in other men is contemporaneous with your awareness that certain kinds of sexual activity between men is deadly. Things may have changed. HIV may be a manageable condition (for some, with the right access to the right healthcare). Undetectable might now mean untransmittable. God, I hope so. But I will never *not* wonder. This is the mark of those who grew up under the sign of AIDS.

Guibert did not grow up under it, but he was victimized by AIDS and served as a warning for the rest of us. We might think of all of his prodigious output, particularly after his diagnosis, as a warning, a call to wake the fuck up.

And what a warning he gave. Guibert kept writing, book after book, taking photos—and more. He made a film, an hour-long film, one of his final works, *La pudeur ou l'impudeur* (*Modesty or*

---

4 I don't have a source for Halperin's statement. I heard it once and jotted it down. I might have heard David himself say it. I don't remember, but I remember jotting it down, remember wanting to remember it. Even if he didn't say it, though I'm sure he did, I stand by it. It's a powerful idea.

Immodesty), and it may be the most powerful case in point from this writer, this artist, about gay and queer damage.[5]

You want damage? You want *gay* or *queer* damage? Then this is it. This is what you're looking for.[6]

I'm thinking of a particular image from this film, an image I could not secure permission to reproduce. It's blurry, grainy, a still from the film, the writer, naked, his back to us, about to get into a tub. Where's his cock this time? Guibert turns his back to us, his body showing signs of the emaciation that will only get worse. Is he ashamed? Is he ashamed to show us his cock now, withered, shrinking? If he is ashamed, it's not enough to prevent him from making this film.

The film is a document, surely—a document, a documentation, a documentary, video selfie as documentary—and it was so very much needed in the time it was made, with a Panasonic camera, handheld, between June 1990 and March 1991, a document testifying to the ravages of the disease. Other images from the film have impressed themselves on my mind, even the painful ones, perhaps especially the painful ones: watching Guibert sitting on the toilet, likely for hours, shitting out everything he's eaten, his body dehydrated, his bones poking through his skin, his head hanging in pain, pain of the flesh, pain of despair.

Pain of the damage of a deadly disease. Pain of a culture that doesn't really care if he dies, that would in many ways want to see him dead.[7]

But also pushing through, pushing past death. Ross Chambers writes in "The Suicide Experiment: Hervé Guibert's AIDS Video, *La*

5 You can find this film, as of this writing, online (at times) at https://mubi.com/en/us/films/modesty-and-shame.

6 In *Angelic Echoes: Hervé Guibert and Company* (Toronto: University of Toronto Press, 2000), Ralph Sarkonak writes, "There can be no doubt that Guibert liked to shock his readers, and his AIDS writing in particular leaves little that is forbidden—to do, to say—unchallenged" (165). The same is quite true for *Modesty or Immodesty*.

7 In the United States, David Wojnarowicz was the contemporary writer and artist who compellingly identified his country as a "killing machine." I write about Wojnarowicz (among others) in my book *Writing and Desire: Queer Ways of Composing* (Pittsburgh: University of Pittsburgh Press, 2023).

pudeur ou l'impudeur" that Guibert was perhaps trying to *outwrite* his death. You can't outwit it, but can you write oneself past it?[8]

"Writing (writing one's death) thus has a figurative status of a prophylaxis: it works, like Bactrim against PCP, to fend off the OI [opportunistic infection] of despair" (76).

"The survival of the writing subject long enough to tell the story of his dying, and then the survival of the subject of writing as a posthumous phenomenon conditioned on the writer's death" (77).

Chambers is talking about writing and filmmaking as though they are the same, what he calls a "suicide experiment" (81)—what I might call, linking Guibert to my own experience, a compulsion to compose, however that comes to one. Writing. Imaging. Both together. Filming.

But not just documenting, testifying, and not even just outwriting death.

Something else. Something . . . more. Something that recognizes that your damage—somatic or psychic—won't quite go away before it's all said and done, before it—*you*—are over.

And then, more, something further, something else.

Otherwise, how do we explain why Guibert spent so much time writing and photographing himself. Not writing *about*. Not taking pictures *of*. But *writing himself, photographing himself*. Even to the end, the very end, when he started *filming himself*, because the horror of it all needed the dimensionality of time as well as image and words to make it manifest, if such manifestation is possible, to others.

But he wanted not just to capture the horror of it. Never, for Guibert, not just the horror, even if the "not just" doesn't make room, exactly, for beauty. But it does make room for something . . . something else.

Go back to the film *Modesty or Immodesty*. The film, a home movie really, begins with bells ringing. So hard not to hear for whom the bell tolls in the images following, the images of a body being hollowed out from the inside. But still, *still*, so much life. We see Guibert

8 *L'esprit créateur* 37, no. 3 (Fall 1997).

dressing, sleeping, shitting, undergoing various medical procedures, attempting to exercise, talking with doctors . . . dancing! . . . getting massaged . . . over and over again for an hour. There's a lovely, moody pop music scene with Guibert in his study. What is he thinking? We don't know, but we *do know* he's there, existing, being.

We see him go to Elba, one of his favorite places in the world, a place of respite, of sand, of writing, of cruising, of fucking. The bells return. He repeats a familiar posture, sitting, head thrown back, legs outstretched, breathing heavily. And then he's writing again, this time with music overlaying the scene, the opening theme from Prokofiev's *Peter and the Wolf.*

And more, oh god, more. We see him taking a dose of something . . . an overdose? Is he mimicking a suicide attempt? Or is this the real thing, an attempt, failed, caught on video? What unspeakable pain, such unspeakable fucking pain either way, to film your suicide, a possibly botched suicide at that. But speaking the pain nonetheless, speaking the sheer living agency of choosing one's death in the process of filming the dregs of one's life.

Speaking. Showing. Writing. Making this movie. Persisting.

Persisting in, through, with damage, a damage that will kill him.

It wasn't always like this.

Earlier in his life he publishes *Ghost Image*, the book Guibert writes in response to *Camera Lucida*. The book has not one image in it. Not one.[9]

Is he hiding something? Is he, perhaps, ashamed?

Oh, he was photographing, making images, making *many* images. Picture books, even. *Suzanne et Louise*, for instance, about his beloved aunts and their odd life together and his even odder relationship to them.[10] But his *writing about* images is *without* image.

---

9 Hervé Guibert, *Ghost Image*, trans. Robert Bononno (Chicago: University of Chicago Press, 2014).

10 Hervé Guibert, *Suzanne et Louise* (Paris: Gallimard, 2019). I don't have space to get into this book here, but if you're curious, check out "Pyrographies: Photography and the Good Death," *Women & Performance* 22, no. 1 (2012), in which Jill H. Casid meditates on Guibert's *Suzanne and Louise*, suggesting that one of the

Why? Why write *around* the image? At the time, Guibert suggests that he's more interested in the photographs that we *fail* to take, the missed opportunities, as well as the images that we attempt to take but that *don't come out.*

The images that *aren't there.*

Modesty or Immodesty, at the end of his life, is *all image,* but it too is about an image that won't come out. An image of a self that won't get out of its life alive. An image of opportunities more and more missing. An image of the damages the lurk unseen for a long, long time, until they can't *not* be seen, until they emerge, demanding accounting, becoming an image that erases the self, and then erases the image of their emergence.

An image of a self increasingly bearing the marks of its disappearing.

But still . . . somehow . . . there.

I lean in close to the screen.

Over or under or around the chatter, the music, the burbling sounds of shitting, I hear Guibert, as I watch him dying on screen, as I watch him recording his dying, as I watch him imagining me, or someone like me, watching him recording his dying . . .

I lean in close to the screen . . .

Fuck you.

So.

I look back at the picture of Guibert with his substantial member and wonder: Did he know he was HIV positive when he took this

---

great pleasures—and a great value—of the book is the way in which it offers images designed to unsettle viewers. Casid writes, "Such openness to unsettlement and not rendering life's complexities in stark contrasts of black and white may give us a resource for ethics" (120). More broadly for photography, Casid suggests "that we can understand the strange time-space of the photograph with its complicated and seductive temporal hovering and spatial traversals between various then and theres and right here–right nows, pushing into our present and taking us back there, as a kind of performance space and event, tantalizing with the promise of the narcissism of returned reflection and burning us with the same of refusal" (123).

autoportrait, this selfie? Is he showing off his penis to us, perhaps even to himself, still in the flush of youth, still looking healthy, the harbinger of his death lurking invisibly within, hidden behind this impressive cock? Or did he *not* know? Later in life, infected, did he look back at this image and wonder if he were already infected but just didn't know? I'm resisting the urge to find out, to investigate, to give in to the scholarly impulse to find out. I bet I could. But staying in this moment of unknowing is more generative. Staying in this moment allows me to experience yet again the kind of unknowing that characterized so much of my youth.

Did I get it? Do I have it? Did he give it to me? Did that seemingly innocent playing around set in motion the particular trajectory of my demise? Should I have kept that cock out of my mouth?

I love Guibert's cock because I see in it all of the cocks that have been the locus of such questions for so many queer young people. I love Guibert's cock because the alternative is too awful—hating it, hating myself, hating others like me, giving in to the hatred of gay and queer men that still to this day circulates like a virus in our culture, a virus just as deadly as any immune-deficiency-causing virus. I'm so fucking tired of hating myself, of continuing to swallow the bitter spunk of self-loathing forced down my throat, the psychic raping that started in my childhood, that ruined my adolescence, that perverted my adulthood, that taught me to despise myself all the more because I myself am a pervert, bent, wrong, turned, like something sour that should be thrown out, filled with diseased semen, impregnating others with nothing but death. The words fly across this keyboard, a frenzy of self-hatred spewing forth from my fingertips because these are the words and phrases and mantras that still pulse beneath my skin, itching to come out.

It is so much easier to hate myself. That's the real damage this culture inflicts.

I can only meet that damage—not overcome, or dismiss, or erase, or even transform that damage—with the love of Guibert's cock, with loving this dead man's cock, with coming to adore something that, most of the time, I do not adore. But I embrace my perversion. I work against my own inclinations *not* to love this cock, to love any cock, because I cannot at this point tell if that mild distaste for the male genitalia is something itself unnatural, an unnatural inclination given to me, fed to me with the heaping spoonfuls of self-hatred served alongside my daily bread.

Fuck them, O Lord, for fucking me over with this disinclination to the cock. Give me today my daily cock, my own and that of my brothers, my many brothers, some dead, many more yet alive, with their beautiful cocks. Give me Guibert's cock, as he offered it up in this selfie, this autoportrait, this autoerotic adoration of self and member, given so that all of us might glory and wonder.

I allow myself, finally, to wonder. And, more important, to glory in it. I am trying to recover, or to find for the first time, the glory of the cock, despite all of the self-hatred, all of the damage that would have me hate my cock, hate myself.

I'm sitting in the car, waiting for my mother, and I notice a cute young guy several feet in front of me, standing beside a van, likely his van, talking on the phone. He's walking around, animated, gesticulating, clearly engaged in the conversation. Smiling. This must be a good conversation. And he's a good-looking dude, what we used to call swarthy, bearded, but tightly so, trim, probably athletic, or at least a dude who takes care of his body, who spends time styling his tight curly black hair. Likely Middle Eastern. He's attractive. I'm attracted. Obviously, as I find myself staring at him, watching him enjoying his conversation.

You're thinking, of course, that I call him swarthy and likely Middle Eastern, and so I'm fetishizing this guy, and I wonder if I am. As soon as I say "I wonder" I feel like I am, like I can't not be, but then again can we ever not fetishize others, especially in those moments when our attention is caught, as mine is now, caught by this dude, caught by my memory of this dude, and I'm rationalizing, you'll say I'm rationalizing, I can hear you saying it, I hear myself saying it, I accuse myself, I'm fetishizing, I'm rationalizing, making excuses for a perverse implantation in me that sees a swarthy dude and thinks yeah, me like, me likey, and there's no way out of this, just no fucking way out of this. I'm attracted to swarthy dudes. My husband is a person of color. Does it exonerate me at all to say that I'm attracted to white dudes too? That some of my most powerful and unfortunate crushes have been on the palest possible white dudes? Does that help, does that fucking help at all? I so don't want my desires to be culturally pathological, just another sign of my imperialist colonizer spirit wanting to contain and confine all of the brown bodies around me. I swear I'm not doing that. I swear it.

Still, I can't deny that his being Middle Eastern, or potentially so, has a point beyond all of this, a point—and I'm getting to it.

Because, as I'm staring, watching this guy's enjoyment, watching as he walks around, gesticulating, lifting his legs, first one, then another in excitement, stretching his legs, the fabric of his pants, his green pants, pulling tightly across his taut ass, as I'm watching all of this, admittedly staring, he notices me, just for a moment, and then again, looks me straight in the face. I'm caught, caught out staring. So I smile, quickly smile and then look away. The smile is to disarm him, to disarm the situation. Yes, I'm staring, but I'm harmless, just sitting here, waiting for my mother, enjoying the scenery, enjoying you enjoying your conversation. I smile and look away, nothing really to see here, it's innocent, I'm innocent, I mean you no harm. Then I look back, and he's still staring at me, staring at me this time. He's not smiling anymore, he's still, standing still, straight up and down, just looking back at me. I continue to smile and hold his gaze for a moment, seeing him through the windshield, him seeing me through the windshield, several feet away.

He then leans forward slightly and . . . spits on the ground, spits on the ground between us. I look away. I prevent myself from looking back, at least not straight at him again. But I see him, out of the corner of my eye, slowly start to turn away and resume his conversation. He's made his point. He's set a boundary.

I recall that, in some Middle Eastern countries, spitting in front of you is a sign of anger or disrespect, or an attempt to ward off evil, ward off Satan. In this case, I am Satan, the evil to be warded off. I get the message, if such a message is to be gotten, if such a message was sent. It feels that way, because he doesn't look back. I know he doesn't look back because, now, I look straight back at him, at his back turned to me, at him turned away from me. And I hold my gaze on him, holding his gaze away from me.

And then I imagine getting out of the car and walking over to him, not to confront him, not to talk to him, not to engage him in any way, except to bend down toward his spittle on the ground, to get on my knees, and then on my hands, and lower my face to his spittle, and then, while holding my eyes up, now catching his gaze, locking on his eyes as he's turned back to look at me, him still holding his phone to his ear, wondering now what the fuck I'm doing, a little look of distaste starting to form on his mouth. Holding his gaze, my eyes turned up to his, I lower my head, lower my mouth to his spittle . . . and lick it up. I lick up his spit, catching some pebbles from the pavement, perhaps a stray hair or other some human detritus with the globule of his spit. Not smiling, not betraying any emotion really, I keep my eyes locked on his, his on mine, as I lick his spit and then swallow. I get back up and return to the car, without looking back.

This is not abjection. I know, I know, it looks like it. You're thinking Jean Genet, maybe Julia Kristeva.[11] I'm the abject faggot, one licking the spit off the ground before the guy who rejected me, who rejected not just an advance (even though there was not an advance) but rejected me in advance, rejected my very being, consigning me to the role of something evil, something Satanic, something to be denied, cast out, unclean, disgusting. Yes, yes, all too easy to say that me imagining my licking up this spit is something abject. But I don't feel in any way abject, imagining licking up his spit doesn't feel abject. It feels victorious. It feels like I have acknowledged something awful, something awful said or done to me and have said in response, "Is that the best you've got? Is that the worst you can do? Well, fuck that. I can do you one better. Look what I can do to myself."

Again, some of you will persist in thinking this is abjection, or maybe that I'm a fetishist, that I want someone to spit at me, spit on me, spit in my mouth, maybe even piss on me in disgust. I don't. Those things do not turn me on, even as I intend absolutely no shame, would never want anyone who wants those things to feel shame for wanting them, unless they actually want to feel shame, and then I think, go for it. No, those feelings do not motivate, do not animate, do not excite me. Others like them, sure, but not these in particular.

11 So much to say here, but see Jean Genet, *Our Lady of the Flowers,* trans. Bernard Frechtman (New York: Olympia Press, 2004), or Julia Kristeva, *Powers of Horror: An Essay on Abjection*, trans. Leon S. Roudiez (New York: Columbia University Press, 1982), for versions of abjection, queer and otherwise.

So think what you need to think. I walk away from this imagination of having licked up his spit and feel not abject or object or even erotic—but like . . . I feel like . . . I am here.

I am here.

Fuck you.

Before I get to my next photographer, my next artist, I pivot (that tired word of the pandemic) through another victim of that *earlier* pandemic, the one still going on (and don't they all, never ending, just becoming tired and old, even boring to those safe from them?).

I pivot through Derek Jarman, who makes his own AIDS film, like *Modestly or Immodesty*, just two years after Guibert's.

Blue (1993) is only about an hour long.[12] It is without images, except for a deep blue screen that never changes. If you watch the film, you face the blue while listening to Jarman's voice tell his story, accompanied by sounds, other voices, music, a sonic space of someone not just going through a life (though not *not* that too) but the bits and pieces of a life assembled through sound to build for you, in your own mind, a sense (if not quite an image) of what it's like to be dying of AIDS. The lack of image becomes pointed, as though the film is telling you: *you can't imagine this, not visually.* Jarman wants instead to cut to some more fundamental sense, something more primal, something *beyond* or *deeper* than the visual world that is so ubiquitous, such a surround, that we tune out most of it just to get through our lives.

So just sound, sound, including his quiet voice, almost mumbling but still articulate. You start to lean in, not fully conscious of doing so, to make sure you hear it better.

And what do you hear?

So much, from the opening mindfulness bell, returning periodically, a reminder of embodied experience, but then also historical comments about the lack of treatment available for AIDS victims, bits and pieces of culture and Jarman's memories—trying to hold

12 As of this writing, you can see the film online in a few different places, such as https://www.youtube.com/watch?v=w-hmuUAmFHQ.

on to something? Then more, more talk, talk about all the shades of blue, coming and going, past and present, and then music, sounds, bells, music, voices, street sounds, snippets of jazz, names of lovers lost . . . then new agey music, disco music, a rundown of the various side effects of medicines, contemplations of suicide, reflections on the death of friends . . . then gagging on taking thirty pills a day . . . and then whispers . . . more whispers . . .

Jarman alternates between the particularities on the one hand of embodied experience, going blind, especially—hence the blue screen, a large blank—and talk of how "hell on earth is a waiting room" followed by "always a discussion of needles"—and then, on the other hand, the abstraction of becoming disembodied . . . transcendent? Or a spirit? He tells us, "I've walked behind the sky." What are you seeking? "The fathomless blue of bliss," leaving the "house" of the body.

He asks us, and himself, "How did my friends cross the purpled river?"

I don't know, Derek. I don't know.

Did you ever find out?

I turn my page to ask someone else.

Mark Morrisroe

Mark Morrisroe died a couple of years before Guibert, about four years before Jarman. He was thirty years old. He didn't live to become the great artist of his early promise, but he has become an important artist whose contemporary fame rests in part on AIDS nostalgia, a fascination with that time and those places in the 1980s in which the epidemic was starting to rage and then the queers themselves were starting to rage in the streets.

I borrow the term "nostalgia" from a colleague, Lucas Hildebrand, younger than me, who uses the term to mark the attractiveness of the energy of the time, the activism, the fighting back—but all in a retrospective looking-back that is not based in any direct knowledge of the time.[1]

The time, one might say, wasn't all that pretty.

What is this fascination, though, this *fetishization* with those we lost to AIDS in its early days, the lost in their own early days? What are we mourning? What did we lose, and what are we trying to recover in going back, again and again, to that time?

Even more, what about the lost themselves?

What do we know of Mark?

Dead at thirty, a performer, photographer, hustler, self-inventor, prostitute, a bullet lodged near his spine, shot by a trick, limping the rest of his life, beautiful still, lithe, loved photographing his friends, playing with negatives, sandwiching them together, creating paint-

1 Lucas Hildebrand, "Retroactivism," *GLQ: A Journal of Lesbian and Gay Studies* 12, no. 2 (2006), https://www.deepdyve.com/lp/duke-university-press/retroactivism-LtuRgipwJG.

erly effects from the Polaroids of his friends, his lovers, his fellow hustlers and druggies, boyfriend of Jack Pierson, friend of Tabboo! (Stephen Tashjian), part of what came to be known as the Boston School, compatriot of Nan Goldin, dead at thirty. AIDS, naturally.

Naturally.

I do not have AIDS, nor am I HIV positive. I feared sex too much, unlike Mark, to ever really have much of it. I grew up watching Rock Hudson die on national television. I've told this story before. I can't not tell it again.

AIDS is my shadow, a ghost image, a haunting, the darker proof, the negative. I am always thinking about it, even when I am not thinking about it.

In *We Are Having This Conversation Now: The Times of AIDS Cultural Production*, Alexandra Juhasz and Theodore Kerr talk about the power of cultural production, including video, during the AIDS crisis, the power of that production to articulate the trauma of the time: "Cultural objects hold information, stories, and also legacies of power and pride, voice, and silence. They allow us to better understand who gets to speak and how and when they are heard. Who is remembered. Whose voice is lost."[2]

Mark was lost. As was Hervé. I was not lost. But I still lost so much. AIDS imprinted itself *culturally* on my psyche. I feared sex. I still fear sex. I will likely never not fear sex, the sexual, the erotic, intimacy with another body or bodies. Sex kills. Intimacy is dangerous.

This is not just emotional baggage. This is *my body*, deprived of eroticism with other human beings. And it makes me think, perhaps, that AIDS nostalgia, whatever else it might be, is in some ways about being comfortable with sexuality and the erotic as long as the participants are dead.

I hope not.

Mark took so many pictures of his friends, his self, early selfies, like Guibert. Posing, often, mostly naked. The photographs depart from

---

2 Alexandra Juhasz and Theodore Kerr, *We Are Having This Conversation Now: The Times of AIDS Cultural Production* (Durham, NC: Duke University Press, 2022), 12.

realistic conventions to stage a life of glamor, however impoverished, of aesthetic refinement in the face of deprivation, of the trashiness of a life in poverty becoming transformed through Polaroids into a document, not just of damage, but of sustained hope for something different. That *trashiness* is significant.

Morrisroe often went by the name "Mark Dirt" and even co-founded a zine called *Dirt Magazine* as a way to signal his low-class background, born to a mother with a drug addiction and eventually trying to make a living as something of a hustler, even getting shot by one of his johns. He felt that he came from *trash,* in fact *was* trash himself. What to do when you wake up and find yourself part of the refuse of the social order? Well, one thing you can do is make trash *fabulous,* or at least die trying. That is a significant part of Mark's story, of his aesthetic, of the horizon of possibility he attempted to imagine and enact in his art.

I can't help but see the photographs, the Polaroids, over which he often scribbled notes, dates, places, names, and think of them as documents of the lost.

But for Mark, they were something different.

"It kills me to look at my old photographs of myself and my friends. . . . We are such beautiful, sexy kids but we always felt bad because we thought we were ugly at the time. It was because we were such outcasts in high school and so unpopular. We believed what other people said. If any one of us could have seen how attractive we really were we might have made something better of our lives. I'm the only guy that I know who wanted to run away to be a prostitute."[3]

Fuck. They don't know what's about to hit them, posing for these Polaroids before AIDS—and they already feel lost, outcast, unclean, dirty.

"We believed what other people said."

I know, Mark. I know. I felt it too. I, too, felt outcast, unclean, even as I tried desperately to hide my dirty thoughts about other boys. I so wanted to escape, both from myself and my early life,

---

3 In Beatrix Ruff and Thomas Seelig, *Mark Morrisroe* (Winterthur, Switzerland: JRP Ringier, 2011), 297.

but just didn't have the wherewithal to run away, to escape into the outcast state of prostituting my own body, which you knew was a better choice than continuing to listen to what other people said, absorbing the damage of their words, if not at times their fists. Or the bullets shot at you.

Still, you're wondering, wandering, thinking you are already lost, long before you get HIV, wondering if you "might have made something better" of your life.

Something better.[4] I hear that. Such pressure.

Then I pick up a book of your photographs.

From a review of his work: "If David Wojnarowicz is controversial, Mark Morrisroe makes him look like Mary Poppins. . . . His self-portraits, enlargements of Polaroids, are the most shocking in *Witnesses* [Nan Goldin's show on AIDS]. The Polaroids look as if they were retrieved from the trash to tell the autobiographical story of an artist who seems to have thrown his life away." So wrote Elizabeth Hess in the *Village Voice*.[5]

The phrase "retrieved from the trash" gives me pause. For sure Jesse Helms would have thought that Mark was trash and that he and all the other queers like him should be swept out with the garbage. But I immediately think of the synonyms, the chain of associations: garbage, trash, *refuse*. I think how refuse becomes *refuse*, a verb, an action, a stab at agency. "It kills me to look at my old photographs of myself and my friends. . . . We are such beautiful, sexy kids." What

---

4 See too this comment in Deborah Bright's book: "Mark Morrisroe . . . also references Warholian camping in works such as *Sweet Raspberry / Spanish Madonna* where the artist cross-dresses as a Latin diva-hustler—a role he could almost appear to be performing for one of Andy's factory films. . . . His angular face powdered a ghostly white, sensuous mouth a red gash, and eyes darkly smoldering beneath their line and mascara, the former hustler-turned-artist puts himself back on the street, this time as an aging queen in pearls, letting his jacket fall seductively from his shoulder in some *noir* pick-up scene." *The Passionate Camera: Photography and Bodies of Desire* (New York: Routledge, 1998), 298.

5 Hess's quotation is from Ruff and Seelig, *Mark Morrisroe*. See also Steven C. Dubin, *Arresting Images: Impolitic Art and Uncivil Actions* (New York: Routledge, 1994), for early analyses of controversial art, especially around AIDS.

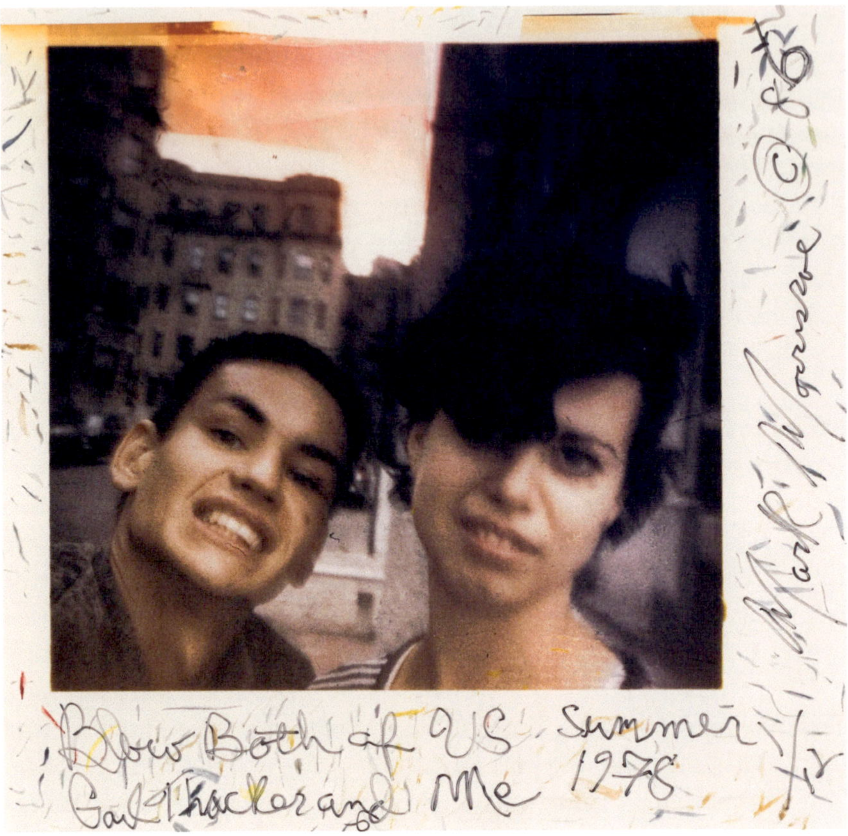

Mark Morrisroe, *Blow Both of Us, Gail Thacker and Me, Summer 1978* (1986). © The Estate of Mark Morrisroe (Ringier Collection) at Fotomuseum Winterthur.

the photographic medium does, especially the humble, low-class Polaroid, is allow Mark and others to see the beautiful, sexy kids they are. Its objectification of their bodies into a visual medium might document their trashiness, but it also creates a distance that allows for a closeness, for a way to re-see what's there: beauty, even possibility, a horizon. To riff on José Esteban Muñoz and his queer theory classic *Cruising Utopia*, I think of Mark cruising the utopian possibility of his photos, seeing later what was once missed—the sexiness, the beauty, the "kids" with all of that word's latent promise of futurity.

But look back at that sentence: "It kills me . . ." There's already a sense of something missed, of a possibility denied in the former present, of something gone, dead. Can the art, even the humble, low-life Polaroid, bring that possibility back, restore it, *retrieve* it? No, but if might offer another line of flight, another life, one in which the former trashiness *is* retrieved—not to make whole what was lost but to transform the lost into something given to others, those who see the photographs *now* (even Mark himself), and take possibility from them. The Polaroids don't just document the trash, the lost possibility of recognizing oneself as something more, something worthy of retrieval (though they do that too). They transform that sensibility into an art of the current—and future—possible.

An art of the survivable.

Surviving. Survivor.

For all the ways others might have seen you and thought *trash*, Mark, you were so oddly self-possessed. You say, "I Mark Morrisroe swear to coldly use and manipulate everyone who can help my career. No matter how much I hate them I will pretend that I love them. I will fuck anyone who can help me no matter how aesthetically unappealing they are to me."[6] This is your declaration to yourself, to the world, to anyone who would, who *could*, listen. It's likely a bit ironic, sarcastic. But your commitment to furthering yourself is in full evidence. You want attention. You will do what you can, whatever you can, to get it.

Your dreams are already of a *damaged utopia*. Not two words that you would normally think together, right? When we think of utopia, we normally think of the bright, the shiny, the gleaming possibilities just over the horizon. But just as often those bright and shiny visions wrap themselves around notions of the pure, the washed, the clean, the spotless—of the trash taken out to make room for that worth saving. But whose utopia is that? Utopian literature is full of examples (think Yevgeny Zamyatin's *We*) in which the pristine and the

6 Reprinted frequently, as in this page from the David Zwirner Gallery: https://www.davidzwirner.com/exhibitions/2021/more-life/mark-morrisroe#

ordered masks dystopian conformity, the horrific disciplining away of anything that doesn't fit.

Mark and his friends did not fit. You can see in Mark's photographs that they are often dirty, Mark's face blemished with pimples, his hair unkempt and greasy, his friends' faces and legs unshaved, their bodies raw. These are not your typical utopian bodies. Theirs is not an orderly world. But it is beautiful—or at least we are invited to see it as beautiful, to challenge our own sense of the beautiful. The bodies pose for us, inviting us to trace the lines of flesh as they curve to just barely hidden genitalia. Mark and friends dress up, wearing feathery boas and silk lingerie, adorning their too-thin bodies in the finery of evening wear that can't quite contain the erotic possibility beneath. Their eyes, sometimes highlighted with mascara drawing attention to how big they are, almost seem to flutter and bat, winking coyly for us to see beyond the dirt, to see beyond trashy "Mark Dirt" to the sexiness, the eroticism, the fully lived-in reality of trashy glamor, of trash made glamorous through a gargantuan act of will. The pimples and the boas. The hungry bodies and a tiara. Damaged? Yes. But still utopian. Compromised and ordinary? Sure. But still utopian.

I said that this damaged utopian is enacted through a gargantuan will, and others have noticed this too. Peter Schjeldahl, the art critic, a real tastemaker in so many ways, wrote that "the cogency of Morrisroe's story has to do with playing the hand that life deals you. If the hand—yourself—is exotically impaired, that makes the play easier to follow. You wouldn't act this way if you had a choice. Or would you? . . . Morrisroe's work is truly glamorous, which seems a fair return on his self-immolation."[7]

Listen to this language. "You wouldn't act this way if you had a choice." And "exotically impaired." Is he thinking Mark's queerness is the exotic impairment? Such strange—and frankly straight—things to say. Fuck. I remember having just come out, sitting with a sympathetic friend, an older white man, shaking his head, him wondering, "Why do those people, those homophobes bother you? Don't they

---

7 Peter Schjeldahl, *Hot, Cold, Heavy, Light, 100 Art Writings 1988–2018* (New York: Abrams, 2019).

know that you can't help yourself, that you wouldn't choose to be the way you are?"

And immediately, I think, oh fuck you, *fuck you*. When I'm walking down the street and see a young ass, tight, straining against its khaki shorts, the proportional globes pumping out the rhythm of walking, I can't help myself from thinking, yes, *yes, I* choose *this, I chose* this, *you motherfuckers.*

Even though I can't bring myself to touch that ass, to ask if I can touch that ass, still: *I choose this.*

I still *choose this. No matter what I have to do.*

Linda Yablonsky says of the Boston School, of which Mark is considered a part, that they took an "obsessively personal approach to photography," constantly photographing themselves, their friends, their circle.[8] Photography as memoir, as life writing.[9] Think Nan Goldin, ruthlessly documenting her own abuse at the hands of a lover, a blackened eye, a swollen face. *This is what love looks like.* Or something, if not exactly love.[10]

We are here, everything, all of this work, seems to be saying, all of the images, the photographs, the prints, the Polaroids, building, building, accumulating. Hard not to think of archives here, but not

8 In Ruff and Seelig, *Mark Morrisroe*, 298.

9 For a very different kind of approach, see Jane Gallop and Dick Blau's *Living with His Camera* (Durham, NC: Duke University Press, 2003), which presents the photographs that Blau took over a period of time during their cohabitation and Gallop's written reflections on them, both from a somewhat domestic point of view as well as what she calls a "professional" perspective, rendered through her astute commentary on photography and major texts on photography by Barthes, Sontag, and others. The heft of the book is toward the analytical, with the photographs bearing the weight of the personal, though Gallop certainly addresses the domestic and intimate nature of the photographs in her writing. My approach is perhaps a bit more split, since I desire at times to perform in this book something of a collision between my professional and personal lives.

10 See Nan Goldin's *The Ballad of Sexual Dependency* (New York: Aperture, 2012). Goldin herself could be another figure highlighted in this book, if she were perhaps just a bit more queer as opposed to queer-adjacent.

only that, surely not only that, not only an archiving, a documentation of presence.

But what?

Ok, here's a stretch. Stay with me.

I think of *The Picture of Dorian Gray*. I like how Wilde doesn't say "portrait." Not a "portrait," but, admittedly, also not a photograph, although Wilde had been famously photographed, many times, and would apparently take up amateur photography after his release from imprisonment in Reading Gaol. But "picture" nicely resides, perhaps, *between* portraiture and photography. And sure, don't you think, when Dorian makes his "pact" with the picture, he *becomes* a photograph, a living breathing photograph; he doesn't change, his image remains static, fixed, like a photograph. Indeed, isn't this one of the key characteristics of a photograph, something Barthes himself points out, how if *fixes* time? For Barthes, the great message of the photograph is that it speaks most poignantly of death, of time past and irretrievable—something irretrievable, like Dorian's innocence once his living, breathing, walking, talking image becomes static and his picture begins to change, to change with the accumulation of his life's story, the picture becoming a kind of life writing, his actions and experiences inscribing themselves into the flesh represented in the picture, much like late Victorians believed that one's life wrote itself phrenologically in your face, on your skull, through your body.

In a way, surely, Mark's photos speak of time, past and irretrievable. I look at his photos of himself and think, *he'll always be just like this. Dead at thirty, he'll always be like this now.*

Sure, his body suffered the onslaught of HIV. It changed. It decayed while he was still breathing, living, walking, talking. It ghosted him. It *made* him a ghost, still breathing, living. We all know what AIDS bodies look like. AIDS wrote its ruin across his body, like Dorian's sins across his portrait.

But before that, before that ghosting, he wanted the portrait, the *picture*. He wanted the youthful beauty. He wanted the youthful beauty of all of his friends. He wanted to hold on to it. He wanted it out there in the world, as well. He looks back on these photos, these Polaroids. *How beautiful we were . . .*

Almost immortal.

Here's another version of Mark and Dorian.

To say that AIDS wrote itself on Mark's body, like Dorian's sins on his picture, is to miss the point, maybe to miss *several* points. Tempting, isn't it? But it can only be part of the picture.

In making his pact with the picture, Dorian puts the weight of social expectations on the picture itself, all of the things one is supposed to be and do—and, more importantly, what one is supposed to *refrain* from being and doing—all of that weight goes onto the picture, freeing his body to pursue what, and whom, and how he wants. *The Picture of Dorian Gray* is a story of liberation, or at least of attempted liberation. It is a story of what happens when someone steps outside of the norm and says that we don't give a shit anymore what anyone else thinks or knows or feels. We will pursue what *we* want to think and know and feel. And Dorian does. Fantastically. *Substantively*, I'd say.

Granted, not without cost. There always seems to be a cost, doesn't there (or so our capitalist culture would have us believe . . . maybe Wilde just couldn't imagine far or deep or wide enough to think beyond the "cost" or the "price tag" of liberation).

In a way, then, the picture, and the pact with the picture, becomes a *practice*. The picture doesn't just document or bear the record of a life lived, however drastically at times, dangerously even, but it is in fact the condition of the experience of liberation. The picture, Dorian seeing how beautiful he is, wanting always to be beautiful, to pursue beauty—the picture and his desire to become it becomes the origin of the liberation into the life lived aesthetically, in the pursuit of beauty, in the pursuit of pleasure.

Almost as though there is not liberation into beauty and pleasure *without the picture*. There is no liberation without representation.

How does this work for Mark? When the world thinks you are trash, when your tricks shoot at you instead of feeding you, when you are maimed but still youthfully vibrant, when you are deemed exotically damaged—then perhaps you take picture after picture of your body, your friends' bodies, your bodies intertwined, your bodies together—perhaps you use your own body to save your soul, to *value* what others would throw away. This is where José Esteban Muñoz is absolutely right, in a short piece he wrote on the photographer: "Morrisroe's photography can be simultaneously read as lush images of people, animals and objects surviving our 'compromised ordinariness.' Morrisroe's pictures visualize an affective world that is an emotional shift from a more realist photographic aesthetic."[11] A shift *from* realism, like Dorian Gray, like Wilde's fantasy—like the

---

11 In a 2013 symposium on the work of Lauren Berlant and her concept of "cruel optimism," Muñoz contributed a short talk called "Living the Wrong Life Otherwise," in which he not only compared his queer utopian hermeneutics with the utopian resonances latent within "cruel optimism," but also gestured to the work of Morrisroe to support his thinking. For Muñoz, cruel optimism, however much it critiques the genres of the "good life" that can't quite make good on their promises, is still itself a somewhat utopian formulation, and one akin (however different) from his own theoretical positioning vis-à-vis the utopian. As he puts it, "On one immediate level, *Cruel Optimism* is about maintaining traction in our presentness, while my writing about the concrete utopian project of imaging queer futurity is an attempt to think and act beyond the pragmatic thinking that hinders minoritarian politics in the present." Muñoz performs in his short talk a theoretical melding of his and Berlant's work, arguing how Berlant's cruel optimism is engaged in "outlining the affective work we do to endure and sustain ourselves during cruel times where we feel the erosion of once sustaining good-life genres" and then how such cruel optimism might also shift into his own work, focused on "enact[ing] certain performances of queer temporality that unmoor us from those things that are so suffocating and damaging in life." In a way, Berlant identifies the sickness and Muñoz a kind of cure or at least *care* for what he calls "the future as a mode of conceptual escapology." At the very least, he argues, his work and Berlant's might usefully meet in "proposing a sustaining sense of the commons that may exist in the future and the present"—however damaged such a sense is by the impoverished scripts and genres of the good life and the material and psychic challenges of performing a life lived otherwise amidst "suffocating and damaging" forces. Muñoz turns to the photography of Morrisroe to offer an aesthetic example of someone—queer, disabled, poor, AIDS victim—working with such "suffocating and damaging" forces to perform, and live, otherwise. You can read that text as published by *Social Text* online at https://socialtextjournal.org/periscope_article/living-the-wrong-life-otherwise/.

glamor of the trashy becoming aesthetic reimagining, and in the process a *revaluing* of what others have thrown away.[12]

Survival.

Survival. Such a small claim, a seemingly meager ask. But it's a place to start, even a somewhat *utopian* place to start: To value what others have thrown away. Just perhaps. And perhaps that's enough. For a little while at least.

There's yet more Mark and Dorian, this time with a philosopher thrown in.

Fiona Johnstone tarts Morrisroe up with a bit of deconstruction. He doesn't need it, the tarting up, but I take away some useful insights from this article nonetheless: "Morrisroe's work is one continuous project of self-representation."[13] Ok, I get that; we were headed in that direction in the last section. But why is the project *continuous*? Does it never *end*?

Johnstone veers through the philosopher Derrida to get to Morrisroe's project and touches intriguingly on Derrida *and* Dorian Gray: "Derrida draws together the themes of portraiture and death through reference to Oscar Wilde's *The Picture of Dorian Gray*." For Derrida/Johnstone, what's interesting about the portrait is its deconstruction of life and death through ruin, the ruining of the portrait as Dorian lives, just like the "ruining" of Dorian's life through his aesthetic

12 In evoking Muñoz in this context, I'd also be remiss if I didn't mention that Muñoz's interest in Morrisroe is one moves across racial lines, with Muñoz, a queer of color, valuing the experience of a skinny, crippled, white trash boy from Massachusetts. Don't get me wrong: nothing is transcended here, certainly not race. But I detect here a way in which Muñoz himself identifies with Morrisroe's *disidentification* from a homonormative world of assimilationist identity politics in his valuing of his glamorous trashiness, his Polaroid sensibility, his throw-away aesthetic of the thrown away—an identification through disidentification as Muñoz articulates such earlier in his career, itself more a transformation of the majority culture—including gay assimilation—as an act of survival. See José Esteban Muñoz, *Disidentifications: Queers of Color and the Performance of Politics* (Minneapolis: University of Minnesota Press, 1999).

13 Fiona Johnstone, "Mark Morrisroe's Self-Portraits and Jacques Derrida's 'Ruin,'" *Third Text* 25 (2011): 799–809.

and erotic pursuits, such that ruin is both moral corruption *and* a "blurring of the boundary between subject and object." Dorian becomes the picture; the picture *is* Dorian. Which is more real? The portrait, or the living, breathing Dorian? After a point, we can't really separate them because what happens to one, happens to the other. What happens to Dorian the subject (the person), happens to Dorian the object (the portrait). And (spoiler alert) when Dorian stabs the object (the portrait), Dorian as subject (person) dies. For Derrida, there is an inevitable ruin, an inevitability of ruin deep down in both subject and object, both Dorian and portrait, that will, eventually, converge.

Then, through Johnstone, we get to Morrisroe's ruin: "The unruly and disruptive nature of Derrida's ruin finds its match in the photographic practice of Mark Morrisroe, in his passion for lying and for masquerade, and in his irreverent approach to both content and medium which exposes the cracks and fissures that underlie the project of representation." Morrisroe constantly playacted, played roles, invented selves, told and retold his history, changed his background—invented and reinvented himself, much like Dorian. And the pictures, the photographs, the Polaroids seem to do the same, constantly presenting Mark in different guises, different roles: seductive, defiant, bold, hurt. Subject and object blur together. Perhaps the photos are mini and even disposable portraits, reflecting back mirrorlike, one after another, different possibilities for Morrisroe. And then Morrisroe mashes photographs together, interweaving negatives, layering different images. Representation doubles, already doubled in its refraction of a life lived on the edge, a life which changes into a new pose, a new set of photographs, seemingly without end.

But can it last? Can it go on, indefinitely?

Johnstone puts the philosopher and the photographer on the same footing; Derrida's thoughts on ruin find a "match in Morrisroe's ruin," in how the artist draws on photographs, his manipulation of them, suggesting a wear and tear, and then mashes together, sandwich style, different negatives, as though the original image cannot hold, bleeding into others, which in turn "exposes" the "cracks and fissures" that "underlie" representation.

There's something weirdly ontological here, as though the ruin is always already inside, awaiting exposure. The cracks and fissures will come out. The portrait will deteriorate.

Of course, Morrisroe is the right subject for this meditation on the always already of ruin because he dies of AIDS, a bit of ruin implant-

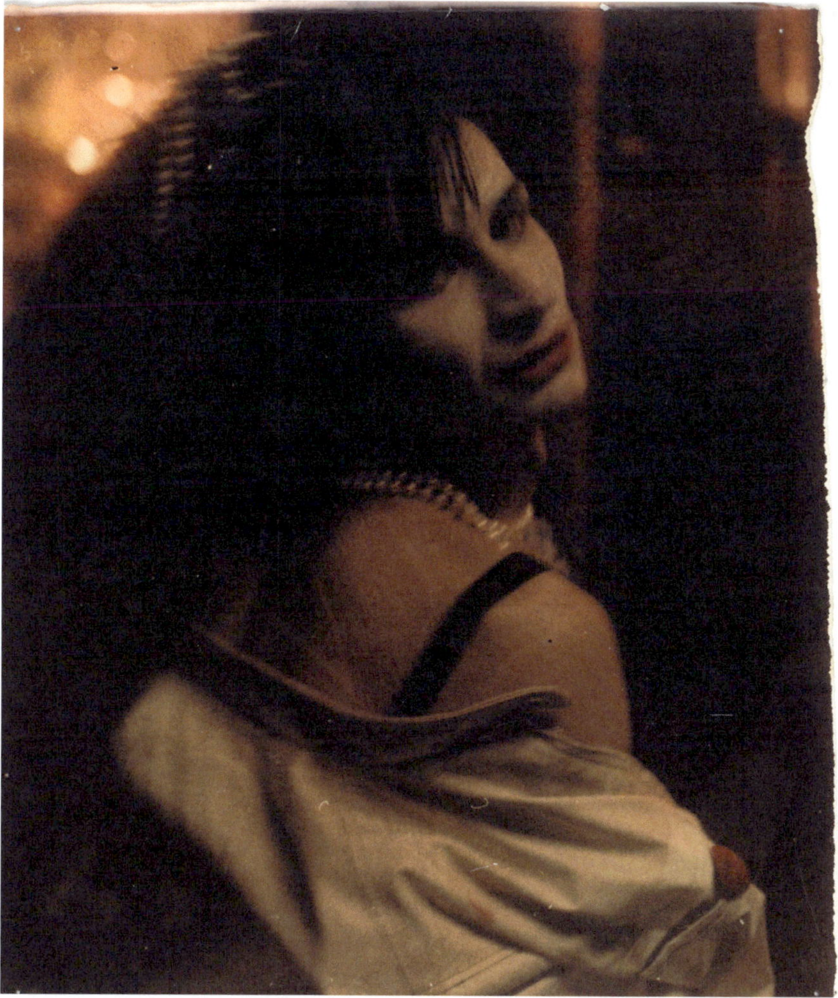

Mark Morrisroe, *Untitled* [*Sweet Raspberry/Lady Madonna*]. © The Estate of Mark Morrisroe (Ringier Collection) at Fotomuseum Winterthur.

ed in him that slowly reveals itself, exposing the body's cracks and fissures, its eventual ruin.

Johnstone tries to situate Morrisroe's work in the larger cultural and aesthetic problem of the representation of AIDS at the time, a time in which people, especially queers, were often eager for representation, for public proof and acknowledgement of what was happening to them and their loved ones; many others, just as often led by US senators and state governors, tried to suppress such representation, denying it funding, censoring it, condemning and disparaging those like Morrisroe, and Goldin and Wojnarowicz, who were trying not just to document their lives but to attract any kind of attention from a culture and political and medical machinery in the 1980s that was willfully turning away.

But there's a problem, no? Are these representations of AIDS about the politics of the disease, or are they about the people suffering from the disease? Are they about the governmental neglect that would rather see queers and other undesirables die, or are they about the lost beauty of the people who succumbed to it? Johnstone writes: "As self-portraits [Morrisroe's pictures] offer an uneasy commentary on how disease often effaces the individuality of the subject; this erasure of individuality was a critical issue in the debate over the representation of people with AIDS."

The disease effaces individuality. But is it the *disease* that is effacing? Is it the disease, AIDS, that damages the body, erasing the individual into yet another statistic of governmental neglect?

Surely, yes, by some accounts, yes. The disease effaces. *This* disease, HIV/AIDS, without the right treatment, unknown at the time, effaces.

Effaces? And by that, do we mean *obliterates*? *Wipes out*? Is anything ever fully *obliterated*? Does even death obliterate? Is *ruin* the necessary result of everything?

Ok, I want to pull back from this existential rabbit hole, and acknowledge much the ongoing haunting of AIDS, no matter how seemingly "tamed" by Big Pharma, for some people at least, for those who can afford the drugs or the medical care or the citizenship to obtain the drugs—I want to acknowledge how, in my life at least, holding these photographs of Mark and his friends, so many dead themselves of AIDS, is inseparable from the meditation on untimely death, on being struck down in one's youth, on the incredible pathos of lives cut short, even when no length of life is promised any of us.

For sure—the seeming inevitability of ruin. And yet—untimely death, the young dying . . . but still young, still young and beautiful in those photos, however damaged the lives, however trash-like, however thrown away.

Still, in the photos, young and beautiful.

Mark might have lived in a way that his body and his portraiture, like Dorian, became one. But the portraits are still here. At least I can hold the photographs, the pictures that prompt my meditation, and that means the lives are not yet obliterated. Not yet effaced. Not what they *could have been*, no; that is gone. But not effaced, for all of that.

So, if not *effaced*, or *obliterated* . . . then *what*?

I think of Catherine Malabou, philosopher. Johnstone too thinks of her—again, looking for a way to get at Morrisroe, evoking another French philosopher, this time not Derrida on the ruin but Malabou on plasticity. Plasticity is a capacious approach to bodies and minds, including both direct somatic experience and the larger body politic. Thinking life through plasticity, itself a metaphor suggestive of movement, pliability, but not without the prospect of being broken or twisted and deformed, permanently—plasticity allows a subject, in Malabou's words, to "project itself onto the accidents that happen to it. And that's how it opens itself up to its own future."[14] That is, as we live, plastic ourselves, we encounter forces that bend, deform, sometimes break us, a very personal experience of our bodies and minds and limits. Broadening out to the social, we can also experience how accidents crack the otherwise seemingly placid surface of norms, norms which are often maintained through the projection of their own plasticity, their ability to bend and accommodate at

14 See Catherine Malabou, *The Ontology of the Accident: An Essay on Destructive Plasticity* (New York: Wiley, 2012).

times. At times, though, accidents and pressures reveal not just the bendable but even breakable plasticity of norms, inviting new ways of understanding our relations to ourselves and to others.

AIDS might, through Malabou then, seem like an accident, one that will eventually break Morrisroe—break both his body and also break the body politic and any fantasy that it really cares for all its citizens. But AIDS is also an accident that is revealing Morrisroe's plasticity to himself and then, through his photography, to others, to us. We see the body and the photographs, marked, Mark-ed, altering, bent, deformed. Johnstone, meditating on Morrisroe, calls this "The Explosive Side of Subjectivity."[15] She uses Malabou's *The Ontology of the Accident* to ask, on Morrisroe's behalf, "What do we look like once we are formed by destructive, explosive nuclear plasticity?" And what can we learn from the plasticity about not just ourselves but the world around us?

Mark's answer, late in his life, in the hospital, knowing he is dying, is to take X-rays of his emaciated body and *mark them*. That is, when he goes to photograph his AIDS body, the body deteriorating, the body disappearing, he does something different, something unexpected. Unlike Guibert, who circulated as widely as he could images of his ruined body, Morrisroe takes X-rays of his body and then draws and paints on them—images that also show the bullet still in his body, the bullet from the gun his trick used to shoot him, the bullet that crippled him for life, leaving him damaged. He offers us images, these interior photographs, of his body, marked—both by past damage, but also *by his own hand*. He makes art of the images of his interior, or at least the interior revealed by X-rays, those photographs of skeletons, of insides, of beneath the flesh.

Of the unseen, the hidden.

Thinking on this work, I wonder: maybe he couldn't bear to circulate images of his decayed body, his once beautiful, lithe body, so instead he offered images of his *interior*. Because maybe, just maybe, however much he and his friends persisted as long as they could in

---

15 In Marco Pierini et al., *Changing Difference: Queer Politics and Changing Identities* (Milan: Silvana Editorale, 2013).

documenting their youthful beauty, what was important to Mark was *what was inside*. Or perhaps what now *had* to be important was what was inside, what was left, before it, too, was gone. The skeleton, the last remaining structure holding up his flesh, it too failing in time, ruined—but still, for the moment, here. And then persisting in the image beyond his own death.

But note: not just the X-rays alone. He *marks* them up. He *leaves a mark*. I *was here*. It's as though we are seeing the upstairs room in Dorian Gray's house where the portrait resides, the true inside, the interior, the hidden, what lies beneath the flesh. But what is revealed is not a soul, corrupt, but an artist, marking, making marks. *I was here. I still am if you're seeing this.*

Mark photographed his life, the lives of his friends, even his own death, not to document them, not *just* to document them, but because they needed to know that they too were beautiful, worth photographing, glamorous even—and worth knowing about even in the process of dying. *Ecstatic* with life, and then even with death. They held their gaze on themselves and each other, inviting us to hold our gazes as well, on their lives, living, ecstatic, even when dying. His plastic body would not just bend, but eventually break, yes. But by persisting in his mark making, he bends our understanding of what art can be, of what it might be. It is not just ruin; it is the emergence of a presence even when the artist is absent. It is the ongoing testimony.

I was here. I still am if you're seeing this.

And Mark would not look away, not from any of it.

And that's so much harder than any of us think it is.

For some, for many, the *desire* is to efface, or at least to look away—from not just the reality of death, of the inevitability of death, even if yours is not so untimely, but from the brute *commonness* of death, from the way in which its ubiquity invites our indifference, even if just as a coping mechanism: "You look like those people, those people who don't care. It is the look they have when they read or hear the news, that look of mild surprise, the slight frown, the very brief pause, a few memories, five minutes of eyes unfocused . . . We

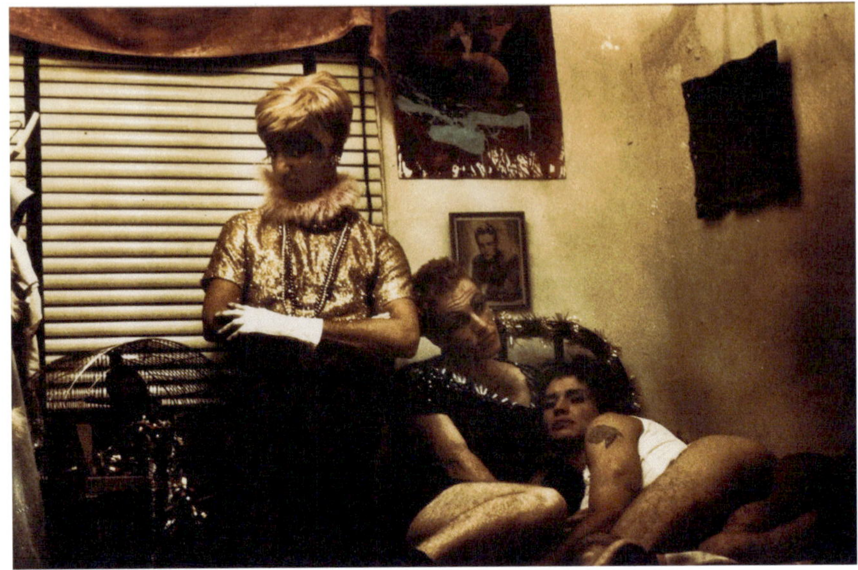

Mark Morrisroe, Promo Still, *'Hello from Bertha'* [Stephen, Jonathan, Mark] (1984). © The Estate of Mark Morrisroe (Ringier Collection) at Fotomuseum Winterthur.

anticipate not death, but the indifference of others to our own death. In some ways, we mime it in anticipation."[16]

Mark would not look away. He would not only not look away, but would participate, would mark the X-ray, would *leave his mark*. He would not look away. He resisted the normative indifference to death, that feigned nonchalance. He held his—and tried to hold our—gaze steady.

Of course, the body is ultimately, ruined. Its plasticity bends till it breaks. The portrait's corruption, even if it has nothing to do with the soul, is all too real.

Ruins.

But is there yet another way to think the ruins here, the eventual damage we cannot escape?

Miles Orvell writes beautifully about ruins and our desire to photograph them, to document the ruin, in *Empire of Ruins: American*

16 Quoted in Pierini et al., *Changing Difference*, 137.

Culture, Photography, and the Spectacle of Destruction. Of course, Orvell is no fool; he acknowledges that the documentary impulse is always already in trouble: "The idea that the camera can best show us what ruins look like is somewhat deceptive, however. Photography is not a transparent medium, and ruins can be made to look like whatever the photographer chooses, within certain bounds."[17]

Photography is not a transparent medium. I think this is why Mark wrote *on* his photographs, his Polaroids, his X-rays, why he played with the negatives, manipulating them.

Orvell wants to understand, though, that the preoccupation with photographing ruins—and I'm thinking this is true, if only in part, for Morrisroe photographing his own ruin—is really about the desire for renewal: "Our obsession with ruins is not only a new pastoralism, an escape from civilization into the simpler world of rubble—a celebration, however perverse, of the spectacle of destruction. It reflects an older and deeper impulse that connects ruins with desire and renewal." For Orvell, we are fighting our ruining all the way, even when photographing the ruins themselves, the sure signs that all of this, including us, will one day pass.

But that's too simple. And Orvell knows it. So did Morrisroe. Sure, accidents reveal our plasticity, even (to use Malabou's word) an *ontology* of plasticity, our bending, deforming, and breaking. But the accident? Is it, too, always ontological?

No. Not always. Orvell writes, at the end of his book, "For the perfection of America—its extraordinary energy and creativity as a technological civilization—entailed a set of practices in land use, energy consumption, and warfare that may have set in motion irreversible changes in the complex pattern we call the ecosphere." Our ecosphere, this little world in and on and through which we live, is plastic to the core—and we have deformed it. It will not go back to the shape it was in. And that, we must admit, finally, has not been an accident. Oh, maybe we didn't *intend* it. Maybe we didn't know, because we really didn't *want* to know. But the signs were always

17 Miles Orvell, *Empire of Ruins: American Culture, Photography, and the Spectacle of Destruction* (New York: Oxford University Press, 2021).

there. The signs have always been there. We just turned away, indifferent, feigning indifference, *desiring* indifference.

Just like so many who turned away from Mark Morrisroe, and others, dying of AIDS. They didn't want to know. They probably told themselves they didn't *need* to know. It wasn't them. That wouldn't be *their* death.

So, *not* an accident. Rather, a desiring of indifference. That's the problem. That's what Morrisroe wanted to challenge.

Mark Morrisroe didn't turn away.

Will we?

Another pivot, this time to the time of the pandemic, a time many of us would like to turn away from, but a time we can't, we shouldn't, a time likely to be with us for quite some time, another time of damage, lingering, a time of ruin.

During the first weekend of October in Southern California, late 2020, when the weather wants to release us from the late summer heat and turn to the gentle fall of a steady seventy-five degrees, a few of us sit, socially distanced of course, in my backyard, drinking wine and celebrating my fifty-third birthday. A friend has brought a vegan chocolate cake, and my husband slices me a hefty chunk, even though I'd asked for a thin slice. Thin. Nothing thin about this delicious but dense cake, its density one of the usual side-effects of vegan baked goods.

We eat our cake, and my mother, herself just having celebrated her seventy-seventh birthday, comments on how much cake we've eaten in the past few weeks. We have safely eschewed larger celebrations in favor of smaller gatherings, and each has had its own cake or other sweet, festive goodie. Vegan doesn't mean without sugar, or the popular substitute for cream, coconut milk, one of the fattiest (if tastiest) substances on the planet.

All of the talk of food prompts Mother to reflect on her career working in childcare, remembering Michelle Obama's "Let's Move!" Campaign. She recalls mashing cauliflower for kids to eat, offering them the healthier substitute to potatoes. She'd sometimes have to drench the mashed vegetable in cheese to get some of the children to eat it, those kids who refused to be fooled by the faux "potato." "Michelle would not have approved," I chide her. She laughs.

"We've all gotten fatter since the Obamas left office," she quips back.

And she's right. Ok, maybe not all of us (my husband has actually lost weight), and maybe not all for the same reasons. But I look down at my belly, the most visible sign of the weight I've put on in the past few months, and think yes, absolutely, I've gained weight. My once solid and somewhat built body, now ruined with this protruding belly.

I immediately think to myself, Why? What's happened? Who's responsible for this? But, really, whom do I have to blame? My once body is now ruined, and whom do I have to blame? Donald Trump? Life during pandemic? Myself?

For a moment, I turn away, back to my cake. I want indifference. I want to feign indifference, for at least a little while.

But I won't be able to forever.

Laura Aguilar

Hard to think of ruins and not think just of the ruins of bodies but of entire cultures, whole ways of living and being in the world. But who wants to think about ruins all the time? And yet, how can we not? I know that one of the tics of my writing is this kind of assertion or question followed by a counter assertion or question and then yet . . . and again . . . You'd think I'm a dialectician, shuttling back and forth between thesis and antithesis, but I never come to synthesis. No, more than that: I deeply mistrust synthesis. It feels, even in the word's resonances, a bit . . . artificial?

I'm already ruining this, when what I really want to think about is this photograph by Laura Aguilar.

I first saw Aguilar's work at the Leslie Lohman Museum in New York, a gallery devoted to LGBTQ+ work. I was with a friend, a sort of lover, however platonic, who was introducing me to this museum. He dutifully left a five-dollar bill in the plastic donation box. I think this is the first time I saw not just Aguilar's work but one of Peter Hujar's photographs of David Wojnarowicz, another two queer artists whose work would come to obsess me.

Still, I'm stalling, stalling about talking about Aguilar's photograph, *Grounded #112*, an inkjet photograph according to the image I'm viewing in a catalogue of Aguilar's work.[1] If I didn't see exactly this one at Leslie Lohman, I saw one very much like it, one of the photographs that Aguilar took late in her life (she died in 2018), pic-

1 Rebecca Epstein, ed., *Laura Aguilar: Show and Tell* (Los Angeles: UCLA Chicano Studies Research Center, 2017).

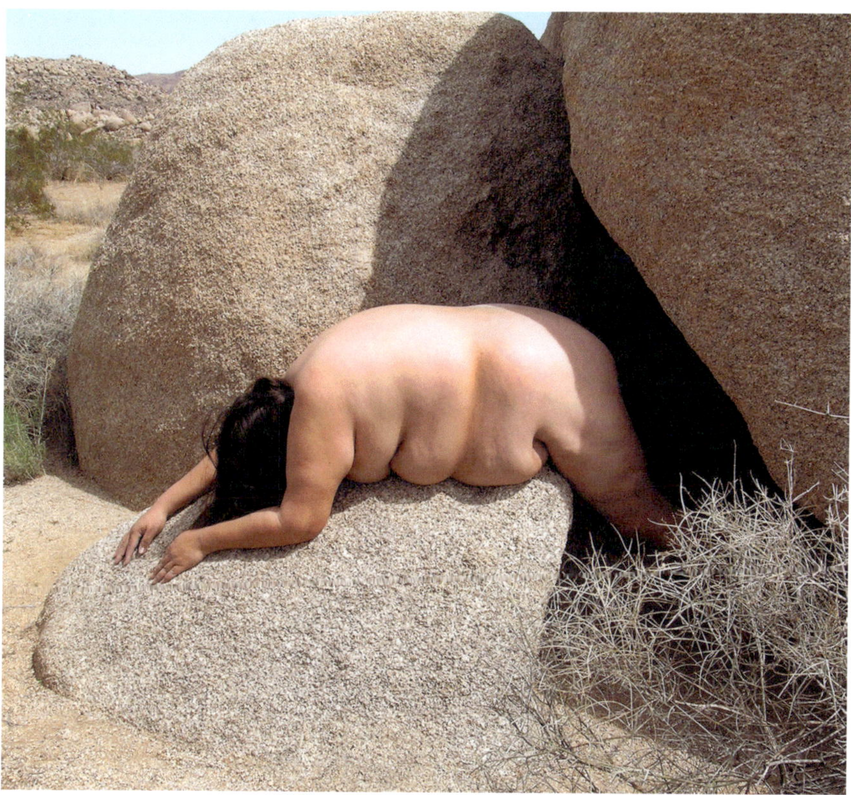

Laura Aguilar, *Grounded #112* (2006–2007). Courtesy of the Laura Aguilar Trust of 2016.

tures that foregrounded her large—sometimes called Rubenesque—body, mostly in these natural landscapes, taken here in Southern California where I live, many of them in Joshua Tree Park.

The landscape, the desert, is a kind of ruin, I guess, though often naturally occurring, like the ones here in SoCal. They may be exacerbated by man-made drought conditions, but, for the most part, they are natural, so not exactly a "ruin." But still . . . difficult to live in.

No, the "ruin" here, perhaps, is less the desert than Aguilar's body itself. Certainly, by some standards, by those of a fatphobic American standard that wants to stigmatize and pathologize large bodies as damaged, diseased, the mark of a life misled, out of control, unable to discipline its appetites—yes, Aguilar's body would seem to some like a ruined body, damaged, one whose largeness is the sign of a life mishandled.

I think Aguilar herself must have thought this at times. How could she not, growing up in this culture?

But that narrative doesn't fit, and it didn't fit Aguilar's understanding of herself. No, the ruin, the *real* ruin was—and is—the legacies of colonization, imperialism, and economic disparity stemming from both rampant European and American capitalism and imperialism, a set of legacies that haunt the lives of so many people of color, including the Latinx people with which Aguilar proudly identified. That is, the "ruin" is the ruin America has tried to make of such people, of its outsiders, of its displaced, of those it continues actively to displace along its southern border.

But even here, ruin isn't enough of a descriptor. Look back at that picture. Some might see ruin, a ruined body, might even sympathetically read it as a body ruined not by Aguilar's inability to control her appetites but by a racist culture that positioned her—psychically and economically—as someone structurally *unable* to take care of her body, a victim of what Lauren Berlant called "slow death."[2]

But even here, again, this accounting isn't quite enough. For that body is, well . . . beautiful. It folds, inviting caresses, even if only caresses of the eyes. It mounds upon itself a plentitude that is its own self-sufficiency, at least for a moment. It swirls over and around itself in creamy delight of flesh.

It is ruin and not, and no easy synthesis is possible. Maybe no synthesis at all.

Many people "struggle" with their weight. Funny how we say "struggle." Like a wrestling match. I actually *dreamed* last night that I was a high-school wrestler, woefully unprepared for an upcoming match. In the context of the dream, I'm not sure I'd even ever wrestled before, but somehow, in

2 See Lauren Berlant, "Slow Death (Sovereignty, Obesity, Lateral Agency)," *Critical Inquiry* 33 (2007): 754–80.

dream logic, there I was, in my singlet, my family taking pictures, facing off against my opponent, shorter, trimmer, and obviously ready to kick my ass.

In the dream, I too was trim—taller than my adversary, since I've been six feet tall since I was at least thirteen, but also trim, lightly muscled. This is how I remember me. This is actually how I think of myself most of the time. I surprise myself when I catch a glimpse of my reflection in a random mirror, belly protruding over my waistband, thick thighs, the dreaded pear shape pushing outward from the layers of subcutaneous fat.

What a fucking slob, I think in the moments I'm realizing that's me, I'm the fucking slob. To be sure, my obesity—for such is what it's medically called—isn't that profound. I'm not morbidly obese (another medical term). But I am noticeably fat. A shaming term.

I'm getting a sense of the "struggle" just writing this. How do I describe myself? Against what norm or ideal am I understanding my body? How do I feel about my body, catching it unawares in a stray mirror? How do I understand that disconnect between how I think of my body, when I think of my body, when I think of myself, and how I misrecognize that body when I catch sight of it off guard?

I play this game all the time. I'm trying to trick my body into showing me its real true thin self. I've moved from just sneaking peeks in public mirrors to turning a corner into my bathroom and suddenly spotting my body, sucking my gut in, hoping to see my skinny self returned. Then I pose, in my briefs, moving around, circling the floor, monitoring from different angles the progression and distribution of fat. I then take out my phone and snap some pictures, documenting different sides, inquiring: What is my best side? How does my ass look? Can I suck in my gut enough to diminish the pear?

Since the beginning of the pandemic, this behavior has only intensified. Nightly I stand in my underwear in front of my bathroom mirror. Every few days I hop on the scale, its electronic numbers blinking toward judgment. Before the pandemic I was a stocky and solid 230. "Not great," my doctor said. But much of it was muscle. With gyms closed, with the heat of the summer, with a little bit of panic eating, I soon crested 240. Now I'm at 245. Sometimes 245.5.

Now 250 starts to seem the threshold, the point of no return. So I starve myself some days, keeping myself at 245. And then I'm 250 . . . and still creeping up.

It's a struggle, all right. And part of the struggle is the rationalization. Note the excuses. But then also note the need to note the excuses. To whom am I rationalizing? Who is owed my justifications?

What can one know of Laura Aguilar, cut down like so many in her prime, too soon?

Dead of diabetes at fifty-eight, so it's hard not to think of slow death, admittedly—diabetes, a slow killer. That can't *not* be part of her story, just as AIDS becomes part of the story of Guibert and Morrisroe that one must tell. Diabetes, the affliction of the fat, the disease of a lack of control, a sweet tooth, a taste for carbs that becomes uncontrollable until you have altered your body's ability to process everything you've put in it.[3] *Slow death.*

But what else? She was born with auditory dyslexia and had trouble writing her entire life. She was largely self-taught as a photographer, though benefited from mentors and friends and their expertise and support. She learned much from the Chicano movement, including its more patriarchal side, and fiercely embraced her identity as a Chicana lesbian. She was large-bodied and wasn't always comfortable in her own skin. She was working-class and mourned her mother's death from cancer.

She loved her people and spent much time, throughout her career, especially in its beginning, photographing her people. Chicanos, friends, queers. Like Catherine Opie, a contemporary queer photographer, Aguilar's initial importance is in documenting the *existence* of alternative communities. Sybil Venegas puts it this way: "From early portraits of family members to the deeply personal revelations of her nude self-portraits and videos, her work reveals her own truth with openness and honesty. Clearly, Aguilar's photography seeks both identity and place, and in the process it draws others seeking similar comfort, groundedness, and empowerment."[4]

---

3 I know this is not the only story of diabetes, but it's one I've been told many, many times—a warning, a caution, an admonition. If you get it, you must somehow deserve it.

4 In *Laura Aguilar: Show and Tell*, 9.

(Writing this, I'm already reminded of our culture's fetish, even vectored unconsciously through its technologies, around weight; as I typed out the quotation above, "groundedness" was autocorrected to roundedness.)

That initial drive toward documentation can't tell the whole story, and perhaps it even tempts us to gloss over Aguilar's accomplishment—and, more important, her *process*, her *coming into photography not just as recording but as transforming*. Venegas herself pushes harder here: "the work evolved intuitively over time as she struggled to negotiate and navigate her ethnic and sexual identity, her challenges with depression and auditory dyslexia, and the acceptance of her large body." *Grounded #112* speaks to that, to the accomplishment of that transformation, a beautiful picture of a large body, full of acceptance (sort of), full of survival (sort of) in the wasteland of the desert to the east of L.A.

My parenthetical "(sort of)" signals that "acceptance," though, seems too easy (even though I suspect Venegas knows this too).

After all, how can these pictures not also speak to so much damage accrued along the way? So much damage that even includes her own AIDS story, the loss of her dear friend Gilbert Cuadros, Chicano poet and plague victim. She photographed him, among other family and friends. He's beautiful, with a steady, penetrating gaze that even his glasses cannot soften. But nothing harsh here in that gaze. Just honesty. Survival.

Beauty.

For a time.

And then there's the even more overtly political work, because photographing and documenting the existence of yourself and others like you can't be enough, even if it should be.

Three Eagles Flying is a stunning photograph, a self-portrait of Aguilar herself bound and hooded between an American flag and a Mexican flag. Why "eagles"? The Mexican flag has an eagle, and the name Aguilar itself comes from an old word meaning "haunt for eagles." Aguilar herself, then, an eagle, caught—bound—between two cultures, two political entities, an imperial power and a colonial

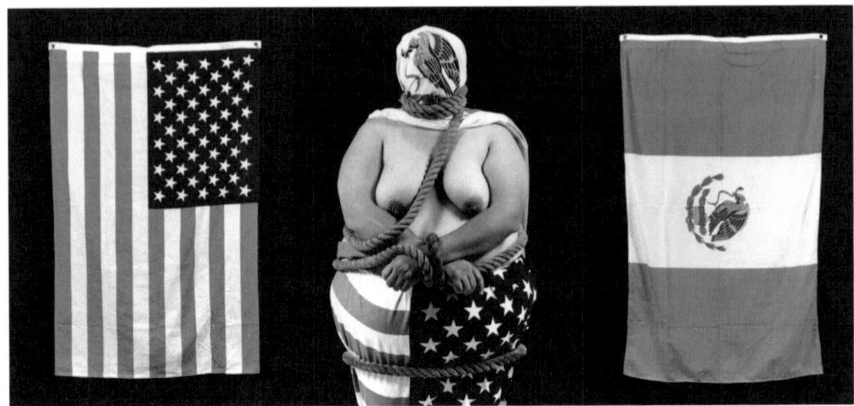

Laura Aguilar, *Three Eagles Flying* (1990). Courtesy of the Laura Aguilar Trust of 2016.

power that has clawed its way to a kind of democracy, paralleling the kind of democracy we have here, north of the border, with an emphasis on *kind* of a democracy. . . . Aguilar, already large-bodied, her hands roped, her face behind a hood, the rope curling around her neck—unmistakable echoes of lynching.

Hard not to think of other queer photographers, Opie, Mapplethorpe, and their use of bondage, work certainly adjacent to Aguilar's.[5] But Mapplethorpe's is so stylized, clearly commenting on the fetish, of both bondage and photography itself as a kind of fetish, a capturing of the body of the other. Opie also plays with fetish in many of her pictures, the bondage equipment part of a scene, even if politicized as a specifically lesbian scene or queer scene, the emphasis on the creation and exchange of complex pleasures in subcultures. Opie's is more political than Mapplethorpe's, I'd argue, because the latter gives over too much of the force of the work to consumerist sensibilities, while Opie wants to bring an underground into the light of day. Aguilar's work, though, is the most overtly, even the most bluntly political.

Political.

5 See Deborah Cullen, "Beyond Face Value: Reconsidering Laura Aguilar's *Three Eagles Flying*," in *Laura Aguilar: Show and Tell*. Cullen makes some interesting comparisons between Aguilar's work and that of Mapplethorpe and Opie.

Her body, caught, bound between two cultures, two nations, bound in the flows of all the history implied and summoned by the flags, histories of imperialism and colonization, related histories of racism and white supremacy. Her body, subject to torture, to damage.

Her body.

Bondage also speaks to vulnerability, which complicates the earlier description of her work and its "groundedness" (or "roundedness," my computer insists), a major keyword for Aguilar's work. Her display of vulnerability, like Morrisroe's, speaks to an ontological condition of human plasticity, but it also underscores how that vulnerability is often *made*, manufactured, exacerbated by political structures. The vulnerability of her naked body in "Three Eagles Flying" is only tempered—or challenged?—by the title itself: eagles *flying*, even if only dreaming of flying in the case of the bound and hooded body in the middle of the self-portrait.

Deborah Bright puts it this way: "Aguilar's body is monumental in its fecund womanliness but is trapped and immobilized by conflicting national identities and allegiances."[6] In-between. Ample, monumental, fecund. Trapped and immobilized. In-between.

No synthesis.

The series "Clothed/Unclothed" returns us to friends and family and others whom Aguilar photographed both with and without clothes. She offers many couples, some groups, clothed and unclothed. I'm struck by one image of a man and a woman, apparently, clothed and then unclothed, the woman holding the man's genitals, hidden from our view, but protected, maybe claimed. Embarrassment? Eroticism? All of this, surely.

And that's what makes Aguilar's work *work*. It's all of this, multiple layers, even when conflicting. Amelia Jones characterizes the layeredness of Aguilar's work as an *invitation*. As she puts it, "Aguilar, by making us work to relate to the people depicted (particularly herself),

6 Deborah Bright, *The Passionate Camera: Photography and Bodies of Desire* (New York: Routledge, 1998), 298.

makes us aware of our own mutability and vulnerability, always in relation to these myriad modes of identification."[7] Yes, that seems right. What do you see when you look at her photographs? Do you see both others and yourself? Do you see our shared mutability, our mutual vulnerability, our common plasticity? Do you want to cup those genitals, any genitals, not so much as a claim on another body (but not *not* that either) but to protect them, to protect the other? And not just to protect, but also then to stroke, to pleasure, to please an other and yourself?

What are the invitations of these pictures that invite us to experience our mutual vulnerability, the ground of our shared beauty?

In the same essay, Jones unpacks the modernist idea of the author as an intentional self representing itself and the postmodernist idea of the author as a "function" (think Foucault, but also Barthes), as in the work of Cindy Sherman, picking up and displaying, then discarding, performance after performance. Aguilar's photographs certainly "perform," staging bodies, her own and others, but I also want to pull back from "performance," since her work cuts to the heart of being Chicana, queer, embodied in this culture. Performance, and also *not* performance. Something all too real, all too crucially aware of the realities of racism, sexism, homophobia, ableism. So yes, performed, and no, not performed.

Aguilar is both, and neither, but *not* synthesis. In-between? She's a self, yes, documented, documenting, identifying, identified. But she's always caught between worlds, amongst different demands to signify, to mean, to *be*. There can be no synthesis here, just contradiction out of which a photographer photographs, a writer writes, an author authorizes the beauty of their being into existence, even while in the light of the damages sustained through the political forces that surround and permeate us and our bodies.

And then . . . and then . . . the videos, all of the videos about the body, about depression, about shame, about Aguilar wanting to hurt herself. *Talking about Depression*. *The Knife*. So much shame here.

7 In *Laura Aguilar: Show and Tell*, 39.

Shame of being colored, of being lesbian, of being *fat*. Fat. *Fat*. A *fat lesbian*.

A *fat lesbian of color*.

In the video *The Body*, having been stood up for a date, Aguilar says she started photographing herself nude, *wanting to feel shame*. She starts to say more, then pauses, then "Now we stop here."

Later: "I started to see my body in a different way." She sees her body in light, shadow, seeing it as though "for the first time," having "its own beauty." A large breast, its nipple distended. Then, "I started to accept myself."

But the shame doesn't go away. She slaps her body, her torso. "This is not something one aspires to be." Then again, she's comfortable. "It's strange how it became . . ." "I tried to work on . . ." She starts, stops, um, and um. "Can't say I've lost weight, but I can't say I've gained weight." "I never thought I would be comfortable with myself." Comfort through the art, peace through the art . . . is such possible? "My body . . . its sags . . . its stretch marks . . . um . . . its shapes."

Hard not to hear the ambivalences in the "um."[8]

Didier Eribon, Foucault's first biographer and a theorist in his own right, offers this about queer shame: "How can the intensity of this shame be understood by those who have never experienced it? How can they understand the strength of the motivations produced by the desire to escape from it?"[9] Shame and queerness have often gone hand in hand with one another in this culture: the shame of being queer, being publicly shamed for being queer, photographs of queers having been used to publicly shame the pervert, the deviant, the *queer*. So much shame.

Eve Kosofsky Sedgwick talks about this queer shame—herself a large woman, a large queer-identified woman, imagining herself a gay man, a spankophile, *queer*, someone also struggling with her sanity, mental illness, depression, anxiety, self-doubt, despite the accolades.

---

8 I am immensely grateful to the UCLA Chicano Studies Research Center for providing me a DVD of Aguilar's video work.

9 Didier Eribon, *Insult and the Making of the Gay Self* (Durham, NC: Duke University Press, 2004), 29. We'll get back to Eribon in a bit.

Shame. Hot fucking shame. Margaret Morrison, channeling a bit of Sedgwick and writing about the work of David Wojnarowicz, another queer who struggled with shame, the shame of a life lived partly on the streets, selling his body to eat, to feel another body, to feel something like love, however mitigated, however faked—Morrison writes about Sedgwick’s shame this way: “Sedgwick sees this ‘queerness’ as intimately tied to shame as a motivator of creativity, and she thinks ‘queerness’ refers to ‘those whose sense of identity’ is ‘tuned most durably to the note of shame.’”[10] Seems right.

Maybe. It’s a formula at least to start with: queer => shame => creativity.

Maybe.

Or maybe not.

Part of me wants to hold back from saying, *yes, yes, that’s it*: queer => shame => creativity. Ok, but really? Is it my own shame that holds me back? My own not wanting to say that shame is at the root of who I am, being ashamed of shame as the root, the groundedness, the plasticity of my being having been bent irrevocably around shame?

Or is what I’m feeling in holding back the imperative to *transform* shame, the need to move beyond it, to recuperate it, to make it something other than itself? Shame through creativity into . . . something else. I’ve been calling that, maybe, beauty. But I’m unsure of this formula, of this transformation, of this (dare I say) *synthesis.*

I think Aguilar was unsure too. To be fair, it would be wrong to say that Aguilar’s understanding of her body doesn’t change, shift, even transform. She gets used to being in front of the camera, gets comfortable, and then says in *Body 2*, “I should be ashamed of myself.” “I must be crazy.” But “Somehow, I got to this place.”

But where is she? *Where?* All we see in the films is her body, nude, fat, sagging, as she turns to show us different angles, a dusky white wall behind her. “Oh my god I did this,” she says when she imagines people going into a gallery to see these images of her body.

10 Margaret Morrison “‘Some Things Are Better Left Unsaid’: The Dignity of Queer Shame,” *Mosaic: An Interdisciplinary Critical Journal* 48, no. 1 (March 2015): 18.

"I'm not jumping for joy," she admits.

But also, "I can't hate myself for everything."

And she wonders, again, what people think when they see her images on the wall of a gallery.

"I don't have answers to the question."

Aguilar has a series of photographs, more self-portraits in which she's naked, holding a pistol barrel in her mouth. She captioned the photographs with comments about art, about wanting to believe that art can't hurt you, but she knows better: art *can* hurt you, because you want to believe so hard that art *won't* hurt you, and that it "pulls at one's soul," this believing, this believing, until you just want to "give up." You want to *believe*, but even art can't take away the sins of the world.

Barrel of the pistol in your mouth. Because the belief can't be overcome. Because the belief in art can't always *overcome.* Because you can't always overcome the shame.

Another video, *Talking about Depression.* Aguilar is punching herself. *Punching* herself. "No matter what I do . . . I can't hit myself hard enough, long enough." Christ, what pain, what internal pain wanting to come out.

And another video, *The Knife.* All we see is Aguilar fingering a blade, more and more intensely. "I think about cutting myself with a knife." Maybe the pain will leave her body if she can just cut, cut herself enough. "I'm not strong enough to do it. But the feelings remain . . ."

"I know there's a different way to live."

"But somehow . . . I come back to this place. . . . In a strange way, there's a comfort here. I've been standing on the edge for so long . . . I don't know what it's like to stand on solid ground. It's frightening . . ."

Standing on the edge, as she fingers the blade.

Because you can't always overcome the shame.

Because I don't think the shame ever really goes away.

I don't think the shame ever really goes away.

For sure, we—all who struggle with weight, which might be every American, even the thinnest among us—we all have our complicating factors, reasons for our shame. The pandemic seemed for many of us the most recent complicating factor that contributed to weight gain. But there are others. (I've made a list.) Mine include the following:

Workaholism: Having grown up working-class and being a first-generation college student, I absorbed early into my mind and body the drive to succeed. And while I was raised ethically enough to want to succeed not at the expense of others, I was brought up under the dictums of Christian self-sacrifice so that I have been completely willing to harm myself in the pursuit of success. This is a toxic combination that many Americans have succumbed to. For the longest time, to secure my place in the professional world, I worked six-and-a-half days a week. I ate poorly. I didn't exercise. I achieved success but at the cost of stiff joints, expanding gut, and higher cholesterol.

Stroke: Eventually, this kind of life caught up with me, and a little over two years ago I had a minor stroke, technically what's called an "eye stroke," as a little golden globule of cholesterol broke off an artery in my neck and lodged itself in a retinal blood vessel in my eye, partially blinding me. Message received. Changes must be made.

Medication: Part of those changes have included a number of pills to lower cholesterol, lower my blood pressure, thin my blood, etc., etc. I also take an anti-anxiety medication to deal with stress—the former stresses of work I took far too seriously and now the stresses of feeling like I'm a ticking time bomb, my head just waiting to explode, because of how badly I treated my body earlier in my life. Unfortunately, these medicines, which cumulatively lower my metabolic rate, also contribute to weight gain.

Pandemic: And then, of course, there's the closing of the gyms and other facilities that I actually did use in what I've come to call the "before." Yes, I could go walking, and I sometimes do, or I could outfit my garage with some weights and contraptions to get my body moving, but, like many of you, I too am listless at times, the overwhelming nature of what's happening to our world making it hard to do more than what needs to be done to keep the money (fortunately) coming in. Hard to think about the future. Harder to think about moving my body in the face of that future.

The Future: Speaking of which, what exactly would I be losing weight for? I mostly talk to people on Zoom these days any way, and I can easily hide my gut. An unexpected benefit of our remote working conditions: In the minds of others, I might be just as thin as I remember myself.

So fuck. Fuck me. Complicating factors, yes, and I know all too well that I only have myself to blame for some of them. For others, the cure is as bad as the illness when it comes to managing weight. So here I sit, a cup of black coffee at hand, meditating on the varied conditions that have contributed to and now sustain my obesity.

I fully recognize that such problems are markers of privilege. Others, far too many others, cannot earn their living by working from a series of screens and email messages. In a weird way, my fat body signals the luxury of my economic and professional situation.

But it also bears the traces of a set of societal values that have been killing many of us, and that nearly killed me.

Traces.

I pause on that word. So many traces. I can trace the creases in my groin, the folds of fat that have formed and that push out my skin into little mounds I can pinch and squeeze, sometimes aggressively. I hold an inch of fat between my thumb and forefinger, jiggling it, telling it to go away, that it's not welcome in my body. I watch these little folds come and go, seem to fill and dissipate and fill again as I try to adjust my caloric intake, vary my exercise regimen, etc. etc. It's a constant push and pull, a come and go. I trace the creases of the folds with my finger and think about what I could try differently next week, what sacrifice could be made, what new diet to try, etc., etc.

But "trace" also extends out to the larger causes, and then to what I call the "causes of the causes," tracing back my health crisis, the eye stroke, to not just the generalities of a toxic culture with its toxic foods but also to the particularities of my life as rooted in that toxic culture: my queerness, my slight effeminacy, the homophobia I encountered early and consistently in life—early and consistently enough that I consider myself a posttraumatic stress survivor, the stresses of early abuse traceable in the folds of fat that now form in my groin as I try—what? to protect it? to protect myself? to insulate my body from the psychic assaults and threats of physical violence

I endured for years as a young boy growing up so identifiably queer in the Deep South of Reagan's America?

I wax metaphoric, yes, and maybe not so metaphoric—the protective layers not just psychological defenses but manifesting as flesh, extra flesh, deforming flesh.

I write "deforming" and hear the traces of a fatphobic culture constantly marketing its stark body images of emaciated torsos as the ultimately desired form while making the attainment of such bodies nearly impossible as it throws cheap, salty, fatty food at us. Yes, yes, I'm shifting the blame, tracing the causes of the causes of my obesity.

I should suck it up.

Then again, pandemic, apocalypse. Who can blame me if I just want to take a break, let the folds unfold for a little bit. Not give a damn about some things because there's just so much to give a damn about right now.

I can't keep up.

Like Aguilar, I too have suffered from depression, more acutely from anxiety, and more structurally from a sense of myself, of *me*, as a failure, of my depression as a personal failing, my anxiety as the deep drive to overcome my personal failings, to outrun my shame, my damage . . . but also, structurally, of the perverse implantation of depression and anxiety in me as part of the consequence of living in a neoliberalized culture of responsibilization, with any so-called social safety nets more a series of strung together holes than anything else, a way to fall through your life before you've even learned how to live it.[11]

Both at the same time.

Aguilar's video work, seen from this vantage point, is more *testimony* than anything else.[12] Testimony, more than just documentation, offers us a way to understand that Aguilar wasn't just *there* but that she too was a victim of a society that either actively tries to destroy

11 For more on neoliberalism and responsibilization, see Wendy Brown's extraordinary *Undoing the Demos: Neoliberalism's Stealth Revolution* (Princeton, NJ: Princeton University Press, 2017).

12 For more on Aguilar and testimony, see Tracy M. Zuniga, "Daring to Be More Honest: Laura Aguilar's Video Testimonies," in *Laura Aguilar: Show and Tell.*

her kind or just as actively tries to ignore her kind into oblivion, so the entitled and privileged can sleep a bit more comfortably in their beds at night.

Testimony.[13]

Testimony, over and beyond documentation, also implies *accusation*. We testify, Aguilar testifies, because what she has documented of her own pain has a cause, has a set of causes, has a *face*, even a set of faces, faces attached to bodies lifting their feet to stamp her out, or to walk right past her, not just failing but *refusing* to see her.

That's why she cuts. She cuts herself to know she's *here*, she's actually *here*, when so many won't even look at her, acknowledge her existence, acknowledge her humanity.

Testimony, even if she has to damage herself into seeing herself.

Damage herself into being.

And then I'm back to the late photograph, *Grounded #112*, her body, her "large-sized" body, draped over rocks, exposed, vulnerable, inviting, inviting abuse from a fatphobic culture, but just as much, more even, inviting caressing, even if just caressing with your eyes, the folds of skin, the plushy mounds of flesh, the intimacy of her nakedness, the vulnerability.

She looks away. I imagine that she can't *not*. She's ashamed.

But there are also so many traces of beauty.

So many traces of beauty.

---

13 Ariella Azoulay asks what the civic duty of the photographic medium might be: "This is the ontology of photography—it always includes more than what one wants it to contain. The photographer is responsible for photography. . . . The duty to photograph derives from the nature of the event revealed to the photographer's eyes. The perpetration of violence, which is the perpetration of injury, is an event that places an obligation on the photographer. Even if at the time of the event she does not have all the tools at her disposal to judge the event, the fact of the injury alone obligates her to create testimony. This is an immediate duty, which typically leaves no room for personal considerations. It derives from the congruence between the nature of photography as a medium that captures a moment and the transitory nature of the event." Ariella Azoulay, *The Civil Contract of Photography*, trans. Rela Mazali and Ruvik Danieli (New York: Zone Books, 2008), 355–56.

I'm going to stay with the traces for just a bit longer, if you don't mind. Let me tell you a story.

A few years ago, teaching a class on "Writing Sex," about the long history in the twentieth century of how journalists and public intellectuals developed different languages and discourses to talk about sex and sexuality in the wake of Kinsey, and before him, of the late nineteenth-century sexologists who started collecting stories of "deviant" sexualities, I remember one particular class session in which I traced the evolution of the terms "homosexual" and "heterosexual"—the former created first to identity same-sex erotic intimacies as a "condition," a kind of innate predisposition as opposed to a set of practices that anyone could possibly engage in. I lectured about how these early terms were not the only ones created to identify acts and identities, and other terms, such as "invert," persisted for decades as preferred descriptors of "deviant" sexual behavior.

I spent some time talking to my students about the work of Karl Heinrich Ulrichs, a German sexologist and early sexual rights activist active in the mid- to late nineteenth century, who coined numerous terms to identify a variety of possible sexual identities, based in part not just on preferences and predispositions in terms of sexual object choice but also gendered mannerisms and body type. His typology of sexual identities puts the contemporary division of our species into hetero and homo to shame, making it seem impoverished—intellectually, affectively, and somatically.

Before the journalist Karl Maria Kertbeny first published the term "homosexual" in 1869, Ulrichs had developed the term "Urning" to describe someone born as a man but with a "female psyche" and who is primarily attracted to men. From there, the Urning could be subdivided into the Mannling (pretty "manly" in appearance), Weibling (a bit feminine in appearance; note the word "Weib," which becomes the English word "wife"), the Zwischen-Urning (zwischen meaning between) for not exactly masculine and not exactly feminine acting or appearing and with an attraction primarily to younger "normal"-acting men), the Virilisierte Mannlinge, a male Urning who appears "normal," and the Uranisierter Mann, a "straight" man who sometimes, for whatever reason, engages in male-male erotic behavior. These are only a few of the types Ulrichs developed, with a collateral set of names for women as well. (See https://

web.archive.org/web/20190627210520/https://en.wikipedia.org/wiki/Uranian#Taxonomy_of_Uranismus.)

What's extraordinary about these categories is how they slice and dice a variety of predispositions, proclivities, tastes, and preferences, but also appearances and supposed interiorities, an individual's subjective experience or sense of self (e.g., "feminine psyche" in someone otherwise who looks like a "man"). My use of quotation marks as I write seems to proliferate because, as I work through the different permutations, my sense of what constitutes "man" or "feminine" starts to wobble a bit. And maybe that's the point. An expanding set of terms comes to suggest, after a while, that the thing being dissected might just be too complex and multifaceted for useful categorization. At the very least, the contemporary terms homo and hetero just seem brute by comparison.

With that said, I won't soon forget the moment in my class about "Writing Sex" when I was describing these different categories, with accompanying pictures that represented the Mannling, the Weibling, and the Zwischen-Urning (among others), and I stopped—quite literally, involuntarily pausing—when pointing to the Zwischen-Urning, a somewhat pear-shaped and pale body.

"Oh my god. I'm an Urning. A Zwischen-Urning."

The realization was partially one of somatic recognition, seeing a version of my body on the screen, but also a psychic resonance, in that, like the Zwischen-Urning, I enjoy the company of younger men, especially younger straight men (even if I don't engage them sexually). And my husband is a younger man, tall, built, pretty butch.

Shit, I thought to myself as I continued with my lecture. I'm a type. And it's a fat type.

To be fair, Ulrichs and other sympathetic (or queer) sexologists thought that the typologies they offered would help to normalize or even naturalize diversity in sexual behavior. Following in the footsteps of other scientists in the nineteenth century who were rapidly, even aggressively categorizing everything under the sun, some (though admittedly not all) sexologists believed that their categories wouldn't just document the plethora of sexual types but rather might show other scientists, and the general public, how regularly occurring "perverse" sexual activity actually is. There's so much natural variety in human sexuality, Ulrichs reasoned at the time, so why are we criminalizing so much of it? Such work and thinking paved the way for later sexologists, such as Alfred Kinsey, writing nearly a half century after Ulrichs, to collect similar data and make similar claims.

A dilemma of typing, however, is that it makes what might once have been hidden a bit more readily identifiable—and then possibly a target. Indeed, the late nineteenth century saw the proliferation of laws criminalizing same-sex erotic behavior, in part because government officials were more aware of its existence due to the research activity of sexologists. So, despite the best efforts of Ulrichs and others (Richard von Krafft-Ebing and Havelock Ellis, to name just two more prominent sexologists of the time), their categorizations served in the short run less to normalize sexual diversity than to create classifications of "deviant" behaviors that could now be managed, disciplined, psychologized, and even punished. In time, the Urning, much less the Zwischen-Urning and other subdivisions, resolved into the simpler binary of hetero (legal) and homo (illegal)—a partly managerial move to regulate sexual activity.

The story, of course, is far more complex than my brief sketch here allows. But I offer it because I'm trying to account for my very real and very visceral response to seeing the image I projected of the Zwischen-Urning—and then identifying with it. Yes, I saw myself in a type long out of circulation, and never really in public circulation. But beyond that, I recognized it as an undesirable type, a type that shouldn't be in circulation, a type I didn't want and certainly didn't want to identify with.

I realized I've been fighting my Zwischen-Urning body for years.

I have been *hating* this body for years.

There are many reasons for this struggle, including internalized homophobia (in general), but also internalized urningphobia (in particular), which is bolstered by what I want to call an externalized urningphobia (in both gay communities and the larger straight world) due to a pretty ubiquitous fatphobic culture in the United States. Having more particularly identified the problem, I can now say that the "dreaded pear-shaped body" (as one friend called it, involuntarily shooting a glance at my midsection) has a particular name, a type, a designation. And unfortunately, contra the best wishes and intents of early sexologists, that typing wasn't normalizing it. It rather made my body type a target of collective and personal—and then internalized—hostility, a thing to struggle against, a demand indeed that I work in whatever way I can to "un-Urning" my body.

And in the before, I definitely tried. I hated my Urning body. For several years, I was at the gym three to four times a week, sweating through cardio and weight training. I hired a sequence of personal trainers to punish my body, to send a strong signal to it that its Zwischen-Urning shape was not welcome. I was committed, even when others mocked me; my physician, who had to sign my release to work out at the gym, laughed at me, saying "We'll see how long this lasts." But it did last. For a good long while. I delighted as my gut retracted ever so slightly, and my arms grew, my shoulders thickened, and I seemed—in my mind at least—a bit more balanced, my chest and gut forming more of a block than the unsightly wobbly pear. And my efforts were noticed, particularly by others at the gym, working out their own bodies, all of us together monitoring one another's progress, encouraging one another, motivating the transformation of flesh into ideal forms. I didn't want to be a Dioning—a straight, masculine man—but I wanted his body.

Now that the pandemic made it so much harder to un-Urning my body, the pear has returned. My chest, shoulders, and arms shrink as my gut expands. I've gone from a tight-fitting pants waist size of thirty-six to the much roomier forty inches. The Zwischen is dominant once again. I miss the gym, yes. I miss the body I was moving toward, that was emerging from my flesh. But I also admit that the thought of going back to the gym is, frankly, exhausting. It's a lot of fucking effort to engage in un-Urning your body, if that's what your body wants to be. Don't get me wrong: I need to exercise, and I actually do miss the kind of exercise that allowed my body to move, that taught it how to extend itself comfortably into space. My joints in particular miss that kind of activity. But, curiously, maybe because the pandemic itself is so psychologically exhausting, I am not missing the tortures of a gym session focused on "straightening" my body out.

I'm not comfortable yet, and I suspect I never will be comfortable, saying that it's ok to be obese. And while fat might be beautiful, and I love dearly some overweight folks, I'm far too conscious, post-stroke, of some of the health complications of my particular obesity.

At the same time, the pandemic, with its enforced break in routines, with its enforced downtime for someone as admittedly privileged as I am, made me much more conscious of my un-Urning tendencies, all of the labor I used to spend un-Urning my body. I'm not at all sure I want to go back to that labor.

The question I'm left with, then, is—*what now?*

Answering that question actually sends me back to the Urnings and all of Ulrich's categories, which oddly survive—transformed, surely—in a variety of contemporary types in the gay male community, namely Bears, Otters, and Wolfs, among other designations that mark a "difference" from the emaciated and hairless young torsos that discipline our sense of somatic self as they gaze, often haughtily, from the glossy pages of sleek magazines. In contrast, Bears are generally hirsute and portly, large guys, sometimes beefy, sometimes plushy—but big and hairy. The opposite of gay Twinks, the painfully thin and depilated boyish waifs that pass for an idealized gay body in some quarters—a legal ephebe, if that's a term still circulating. If buff muscled gays (think 1970s "clone" performing masculinity to the nth degree) are your Mannling Urnings and softly femme Twinks are your Weibling Urnings, then Bears are your Zwischen-Urnings. Granted, the requirement that the Zwischen-Urnings be interested in young men isn't universally shared among contemporary Bears (present company excluded). But the somatic type seems spot on: somewhere between masculine and feminine, big and hairy enough to satisfy the requirements of the former but soft and round enough to qualify for the latter.

That in-between is clearly the zone I'm in, the one my pandemic body has made camp in, the territory I currently occupy.

The good news for me is that having a "type" in the contemporary gay world means that there are people who want my body. After all, "types" only really exist as a form of marketing now, a way to identify bandwidths of attraction, as well as a commodity category for vendors to hawk various paraphernalia and clothing to those wishing to further accentuate their identification. In full disclosure, I actually have a "Bear Pride" top, a large black T-shirt with the Bear Pride Flag (in manly browns and tans) emblazoned on the front. I've read some trashy gay books about Bears (I recommend Wayne Hoffman—woof!). And I've seen some of the apps that gay men use for random hookups, apps designed specifically for Bears looking for local love, with names like GROWLr and Grizzly.

The bad news for me is, well, a lingering internalized bearaphobia (the contemporary version of Urningphobia, particularly Zwischen-Urningphobia). I did not grow up a Bear, even as I have clearly grown into a Bear. In fact, I used to be a Twink. A college gal pal once even complained that I had more of a figure than she had. I was super thin, relatively hairless, and more than a little on the fey side. That all started to change after I hit thirty, with my latent Urning waiting to assert himself (or themself?). My transformation into a Zwischen-Urning has only solidified with the passing of time, various health issues, and now the pandemic. My resulting cognitive dissonance can be acute: I pass a mirror (or, as I describe above, narcissistically dawdle in front of one) and wonder who that Bear is. Where did his Twink body go?

I'm far past the point where I personally am tempted to use the apps to find confirmation in the adoration of a Bear hunter. But I appreciate the men who do find this body (note how I can't quite yet call it mine) attractive. One cute young cub in his late twenties approached me after a talk I gave and asked if I was single. (He was so sweet!) I'm not in any way bragging when I say that such things happen more frequently than I acknowledge; my husband (who calls me "husbear") is always pointing out men who are checking me out. The attention always surprises me. This isn't the body I wanted, so why should anyone else?

And yet, my husband does. And the cub attending my talk. And the barista at the coffeeshop I like to go to, in part because I know the young man—an otter, hairy but slimly built—looks at me with pleasure whenever I walk in, his eyes peeking out over his mask, appreciating me. But is this kind of external validation—however lovely—enough? Is it ever enough? Of all of the things that I've experienced during the pandemic, the full settling in of my Zwischen-Urning body is among the most personally distressing. And yes, I recognize the fullness of the privilege I have in saying that. I have time and means to bemoan my body. Many others don't.

With that said, the lockdown afforded me the chance to think about my body in ways that I've never thought of it before, to regret things I didn't do in the "before." No, not go the gym more. Not diet. Not punish the emerging Urning further. But rather, not going to a Bear retreat, to the Lazy Bear week at Guerneville, just north of San Francisco, to the even more famous Bear Week in Provincetown. These are large celebrations of large, hirsute gay men, dancing, partying, frolicking with one another. As for me, no need to hook up, or experience sexual validation. But maybe being around enough people who seem to love their bodies . . .

Who at least seem to.

Seem to.

I hope they do. Because I can't not hear Laura Aguilar, *Talking about Depression 2*: "I have always felt I shouldn't be here. . . . I don't have that right to be alive."

And then something remarkable. She talks about being depressed in *Untouched Landscape*, talks about being so incredibly depressed, and then she sees one of her photographs, talks about seeing one of her photographs in which she sees herself . . . *content*, in some kind of peace. One of her own photographs.

"A moment of stillness."

That's how she sees herself in her own photograph, if only for a moment.

And then I see her, photographing herself in Joshua Tree National Park, the body, what she calls the vast untouched landscape of her body, *her* body, her *body*, round as the stones around her, the large stones washed round with time.

Beauty. Beauty in the midst of so much desert, so much damage.

An Interlude on the Beautiful in the Midst of Damage

All of this talk about beauty prompts me to ask what I mean by that, what is actually *beautiful.* Too many possible answers, yes. But there's something about beauty, about the aesthetic realm, that these photographers keep coming back to, even when they are working with what, in some contexts, might be considered very much *un*aesthetic, very much *not* beautiful. To be sure, thinking of Guibert and Morrisroe, AIDS isn't beautiful; in fact, one of the more powerful circulating symbolic markers of AIDS is its gross disfigurement of the body, the skin, the face. But even here, in Guibert's hands, and Morrisroe's, and then too Aguilar's, thinking of her body and her hatred of it at times— perseverance, survival, defiance all signal a kind of beauty, a persistence to think, find, feel the beautiful.

I was here.

For sure, a lot of how you see that beauty depends on *who* is looking, and *how*. And *why*. And to what ends. And to what imagined *possibilities.*

Maybe the questions, then, that I'm wanting to ask of beauty are these: What does beauty *do*? What do we want—or need—it to do? What *can* it do, especially in the midst of damage?

I evoked Elaine Scarry earlier and the notion of the inarticulable nature of pain, and I could return to her again on what pain has to do with damage, but I must admit that I'm a little more taken with Scarry on beauty, specifically with her short, manifesto-like book *On*

Beauty and Being Just.[1] Scarry makes powerful claims for beauty, which, she suggests (in a treatise that seems like what a Platonic dialogue would be like if it was just Plato talking to us, a monologue rife with skepticism about beauty and deep feeling) has been given a hard time by philosophers, treated as something insubstantial, fleeting, even trivial.[2] At worst, beauty can distract us from the things that really matter, like injustice or inequity. But for Scarry, beauty "is, at the very least, innocent of the charges against it, and it may even be the case that far from damaging our capacity to attend to problems of injustice, it instead intensifies the pressure we feel to repair existing injustices" (57). We see something, something beautiful, and it moves us, and we . . . what? . . . want a better world, want to work toward a better world, all in the hopes of preserving, furthering, cultivating beauty, the experience of the beautiful?

The logic is fetching, to say the least. Even more, how can I *not* respond to such a sentence, with a variant of my keyword—damaging—appearing right in the middle of it? No, far from damaging, Scarry contends, beauty "seems to place requirements on us for attending to the aliveness or (in the case of objects) quasi-aliveness of our world, and for entering into its protection" (90). Scarry wants to defend the beautiful because it can also generate *more* beauty, leading (in her optimistic view) to *more* attentiveness, *more* opportunities to cultivate protectiveness, care. The argument starts to seem obvious:

> And surely what we should wish is a world where the vulnerability of the beholder is equal to or greater than the vulnerability of the person beheld, a world where the pleasure-filled tumult of staring is a prelude to acts that will add to the beauty already in the world—acts like making a poem, or a philosophic dialogue, or a divine comedy; or acts like repairing an injury or a social injustice (74–75).

---

1 Elaine Scarry, *On Beauty and Being Just* (Princeton, NJ: Princeton University Press, 1999).

2 In the interest of fairness, Scarry lays out the arguments against beauty—which, as she summarizes, may be a capacity for "preoccupying our attention, distract[ing] attention from wrong social arrangements." Moreover, if "we stare at something beautiful," then "our act is [potentially] destructive to the object" (ibid., 58).

Surely, what *should* we wish other than this? More personally, how can I not love "pleasure-filled tumult of staring?" How often have I *not* stared at some random behind, some fleshy posterior walking ahead of me, and been filled with something like joy, an animating jolt of pleasure in being alive, in being able to walk behind a lovely behind? How could I not then want to repair the injuries and injustices of the world, or at least wish them ameliorated enough for me—and any others—to continue to enjoy this sight?

The spirit—the animated spirit—is there. But what repair, what actual repair, can be done? What can repair the damage done to oneself, even as one delights in the beholding of a beautiful behind?

It's 1984 and I am sixteen years old, about to watch David Lynch's film *Dune*. I had, the year before, read the novel in anticipation of the film's release. I was a young nerd, interested in science fiction and fantasy, in no small part because they provided a means of escape from the intense homophobic bullying I encountered as an all too easily recognizable proto-queer kid: tall but gangly, thin and cross-eyed, a bit too femme and introverted to be anything other than, in the early '80s of Reagan's America in the Deep South of coastal Louisiana, a fag, faggot, sissy, queer. Fantasy and SF, reading matter I all but stumbled into, provided escape, a way of imagining myself into other landscapes where the alien and strange weren't always cause for alarm but just as often cause for wonder and excitement.

Surely, even in imaginative fiction, the alien and strange can be monstrous, and *Dune*, while absent actual aliens, was full of monstrous humans doing monstrous things to one another. A vast, epic narrative of interstellar politicking and economic conflict, with "great houses" pitted against one another for control of one planet, the only source of a mysterious spice that enables interstellar travel and offers hallucinogenic glimpses of the future (think, metaphorically, of something that is both oil and LSD, and you'll get some of the preoccupations of this mid- to late-twentieth-century story), *Dune* was gripping reading. Even more so for me because, right smack dab in the middle of the narrative, the central villain, the obese Baron Vladimir Harkonnen, amidst plotting and planning the downfall of his enemies in the most evil and dastardly ways, offhandedly tells one of his minions to bring a boy to his room, and to make sure he's well drugged.

Little skinny proto-queer teen Jonathan had to read the passage over and over, several times. I had not seen before such a bald and blatant reference to same-sex sexual behavior—not in anything I had read up to that point. And while the scene is clearly coded as signaling the Baron's evil, his degeneracy, it struck me as exciting because I was given a glimpse into a kind of sexual activity that I had started groping toward in my mind but otherwise didn't know how to imagine or picture. Remember: this is the early '80s, the Deep South, a time and place devoid of the many, many more images of queer and trans identity and activity that we can see today. And when we did see it in in that time and place, it was almost always, as in the case with *Dune*, coded as marking something very, very bad.

All that coding aside, I couldn't wait to see how—if—such a scene would be handled in the film version of the novel. And I was hardly disappointed. It's a supremely delicious scene, worth watching. One commentator describes it this way:

> After a passionate monologue about how he will seize power, the villain, played by a menacing Kenneth McMillan, approaches a young slave boy. He then rips out his heart plug, a gruesome device invented for the movie that seems to keep slaves in line through the constant threat of death. The boy begins to rapidly bleed out through his translucent uniform as the Baron embraces him. Blood sprays across the wall as the music swells. Other Harkonnen men watch voyeuristically during the act; some are reluctant, some are impassive, and others are interested. Feyd, played by Sting, grins manically at the climax, as though sharing the sadistic lust of his rapacious uncle.[3]

Images from this scene stayed with me a long, long time. Surely, as I've noted, the Baron's homoeroticism is meant to signal his evilness—a move reminiscent of the commercially enforced mandate throughout much of the mid-twentieth century in the pulp novel publishing business only to print works about queers that ended with their suicide or death. That rhetoric—linking queerness to the pathological and to death—seemed in the 1980s to gain particular force with the advent of the AIDS crisis,

3 See Bessie Yuill, "*Dune* | Frank Herbert's Homophobia, Baron Harkonnen, and Queer Menace," *The Companion*, February 2023, https://www.thecompanion.app/dune-baron-harkonnen-queer-menace-and-frank-herberts-homophobia/.

in which the visible deformations of advanced HIV disease seemed (for some) to point metonymically and unequivocally to an interior rot, a deep internal pathology of soul and psyche. Witness the images of Rock Hudson, the first major star to announce publicly his illness from AIDS—and his homosexuality. Some commentators on the film version of *Dune* see in the 1984 film itself a kind of congruence between the presentation of the queerly evil Baron Harkonnen and the physical devastations of AIDS:

> So it's entirely possible that HIV was the intentional subtext of the movie, especially in scenes where the Baron's doctor tends to his skin. Working on the Baron with needles, the doctor and his assistant send mysterious fluids pumping through a nearby glass vessel. "You are so beautiful, my Baron. Your skin, love to me. Your diseases lovingly cared for, for all eternity," he promises the leader with slavish affection. Besides the homoerotic image of the doctor whispering intimately into his ear, referring to Macmillan's obviously mascu line villain as "beautiful," contemporary audiences may have been alarmed by the reference to "diseases." The words "for all eternity" are particularly key: like vampirism, like AIDS, whatever the Baron has is a lifelong condition.[4]

Interestingly, Denis Villeneuve's 2021 version of *Dune* removes the visual rhetorics of queer pathology, leaving behind in its portrayal of the Baron only his corpulence because, hey, fat shaming is still most definitely in vogue.[5] In an interview with *Vanity Fair,* Villeneuve maintains that "as much as I deeply love the book, I felt that the baron was flirting very often with caricature. And I tried to bring him a bit more dimension."[6]

---

4 Ibid.

5 Some more thoughts from Yuill: "It's worth noting that whilst Denis Villeneuve has thus far done away with the sexual sadism of Lynch's incarnation, he has—if anything—leaned more heavily into the vampiric imagery, with the ghoulishly grey Harkonnen (Stellan Skarsgård)'s robes trailing below him as he rises on his suspender belt. Queerness is then inescapably part of the subtext and once the Harkonnen spring their trap, homoeroticism is dragged firmly into the fore as he looms above the very paralyzed and very naked Duke Leto (Oscar Isaac). At one point the Baron is framed from behind, gorging himself with food, his head level with Leto's groin."

6 See Robert Vaux, Averie Watson, and Arthur Goyaz, "*Dune*: How Villeneuve's Film Handles Baron Harkonnen's Sexuality," *CBR*, November 2021, https://

I have to admit that, however repugnant such rhetorical coding is in both the original novel and in Lynch's film (paralleling, I might add, Frank Herbert's own homophobia, and his sundering of a relationship with a gay son who then himself died of AIDS), I'm kinda sorta with the disappointed fans. Yes, yes, I get why Villeneuve couldn't portray the Baron as too queerly evil, and I appreciate the cultural advances we've made in queer representations. And yet, and yet, those early images were important to me—in part because they were some of the few mass cultural images I had that depicted even the possibility of same-sex sexual engagement. More important, if twistedly, they depicted a very powerful and influential figure as having those interests. My own interest in the Baron was perhaps ultimately less about identification; instead, it was a recognition of the appeal of a certain kind of excitation. No, that's not quite right. It was how the depiction of an excitation, however rhetorically pathologized, could nonetheless open up the possibility that one could be excited in certain other ways. And that one might also be powerful and entertain such excitations was all the more thrilling to a pretty powerless young sissy nerd in the Deep South of Reagan's 1980s.

In a way, I was reading the rhetorical force of the scene all wrong. I was becoming excited about possibilities that were not intended to excite positively but rather horrify negatively. The rhetoric wasn't working for me, not entirely. For sure, I understood that the queernesses depicted were supposed to be understood negatively But the depictions, so artfully and powerfully rendered, also positively excited me with the possibility that one might pursue same-sex desires, and powerfully so. What excited me was an aesthetic experience—and an aesthetic experience that I could perceive differently than intended.

---

www.cbr.com/dune-2021-handles-baron-harkonnen-sexuality/. And more: "Any mentions of incest and pedophilia have been removed from the script. However, the baron, played by Kenneth McMillan, is still extremely predatory and a very grotesque character. In one scene, Baron Harkonnen physically attacks and kills a young man. The baron embraces the young man as he does this, implying romantic or sexual feelings towards his victim. Although the baron is not openly confirmed as gay in the 1984 movie, the subtext makes it incredibly clear that this scene was meant to enforce the harmful stereotype of older gay men displaying predatory behavior towards younger straight men."

Yes, I'm aware that I'm reading a scene of rape and murder radically against the grain—not only against the grain in which it was intended to be read, but also pretty provocatively for how any scene of rape and murder should be read. In my defense, I'll argue that when your resources are meager, you use what you can. And I had enough to go on with this scene to then feel emboldened to seek out other kinds of depictions of queerness.

But this scene—both in the novel and in the film—was a turning point for me. Its rhetorical failure to convince me of the fundamental pathology of queerness was made possible, I argue, by its aesthetic forcefulness, particularly in Lynch's adaptation of the scene. After all, the scene, in addition to being generally thrilling, deploys mimetic desire through Feyd's/Sting's approving leer to validate the Baron's perversities. The excitation of horror it intends can easily be turned to neighboring forms of (less awful) excitation.

Sifting this experience through the work of Jacques Rancière, I might argue that the "distribution of the sensible" enacted in the film—literally embodied in the set, the color palette, the lighting, the scene design, the costuming, the makeup, the accompanying music, all over and beyond the plot and dialogue—creates a parallel between the Baron's villainy and his perversity; his very real and oozing sores are the Dorian Gray-like manifestation of his interior moral rot. For Rancière, the "distribution of the sensible"—or the range of sensations and excitations that we are culturally conditioned to understand as acceptable, allowable, even legibly human—is at the heart of what holds people together. That distribution is not so much a set of articulable values (though those are not unimportant, surely) but, even more fundamentally, a way of perceiving the world, a set of shared sensibilities, with an emphasis on how we collectively sense and perceive. This understanding of aesthetics as the distribution of the sensible is inevitably also political in how it invites and excludes participation in communities—and what that community can possibly envision and imagine about itself, as well as the limits of what should be imagined. Following Rancière then, the aesthetics of *Dune* seemed to have been designed to bolster the larger cultural rhetoric of anti-queerness; the ordering of sensibility around the Baron channels and reenforces the homophobia of the 1980s. Watching this scene in 1984, I was supposed to be learning the boundaries of the community (who belongs) and who may speak in and for it.

But while I could intuit (if not name) the intertwining of the aesthetic and rhetorical intentionality here (so pervasive was it in the distribution of the sensible of the time), the power of the scene aesthetically bled excitation, enticement, even a kind of seduction. If I'm pathological, my young self was saying to himself, then at least I can be powerfully so.

Later in life, I would come to formulate this early feeling as a more articulate sense of resistance: When your entire culture is pathological, is it not better to live in a pathological relationship to it? Why not be the evil queen if that's the role assigned to you? But in the moment, my own "reading"—my response at an affective level—to the Baron's scene was one less of horror but, if not quite recognition, at least acknowledgment that being a little sissy faggot didn't mean I had to be without power. Kandice Chuh argues that one of the most interesting dimensions of "aesthetic inquiry [is that it] provides entry to the apprehension of illiberal, uncommon sensibilities."[7] And that, I argue, is one way to understand what was happening to me aesthetically in that theater, and in the months and even years to come.[8]

7 Kandice Chuh, *The Difference Aesthetics Makes: On the Humanities "After Man"* (Durham, NC: Duke University Press, 2019), 3.

8 Different theorists have approached this work in aesthetics for its more overtly political dimensions, such as David Lloyd, who argues that since Friedrich Schiller's late Enlightenment, with the early Romantic connection of aesthetics and the creation of the liberal subject, we have underestimated the power of the aesthetic in forming not just political sensibilities but even certain kinds of political hegemony. Critiquing Schiller's understanding of aesthetics as the invitation to the "play" of contemplation, Lloyd argues instead that "aesthetic reflection does not contemplate its objects for the sake of sheer delight. It judges, and judges of the human: The terms put in play by aesthetics establish the set of discriminations and distributions by which the Savage comes to be distinguished from the civil subject, the partial and particular human from the universal Subject, and the 'pathological' or suffering, needing, desiring human from the ethical human Subject. Aesthetics from its inception has been a regulative discourse of the human" (3). Lloyd's use of the word "distribution" is pointed. He understands the attractions of Schillerian play and "disinterested contemplation," the possibility of aesthetic experience in opening up "a domain of creativity and imagination in which we enjoy the freedom denied to us in the actual world of domination or heteronomy. [In which we] . . .enjoy the anticipation of a world emancipated from coercion and arbitrary constraint" (10). Lloyd just as pressingly maintains that "Artworks, above all, charged as they are with the burden of subjective and particular articulations of social life, cannot but

To borrow again from Rancière, it was the beginning of my emancipation, the beginning within me of "the dismantling of the old distribution of what could be seen, thought and done," and my first conscious steps toward reconfiguring "the landscape of what can be seen and what can be thought is to alter the field of the possible and the distribution of capacities and incapacities."[9] For sure, I would, in time, be compelled by the rhetorics of ACT UP and other queer activists, and would, in time, develop my own rhetorical stances to combat homophobia and promote sexual and gender equality. But what was important as well, in its own way, was this aesthetic encounter, this aesthetic entry that allowed even for the *possibility* of feeling a rearrangement of the homophobic distribution of the sensible. I'm not sure the pro-queer rhetorics I later encountered would have made sense without this early aesthetic experience, or something akin to it.

For all of that, though—for all of that theorizing to understand my early attraction to the scenes with the Baron—I'm still left with the problem of violence, the violence in the scene, and the eroticization of such violence, of damages done to others in the pursuit of pleasures.

Violence. Damage. The erotic.

Where do I think these things together, over and beyond my theoretical rationalization of my initial attraction to their intertwining?

give voice to the painful grappling of individuals and communities with the coercive constraints that everywhere confront their efforts at undominated living. As such, however, rather than representing a sphere of freedom, they bear the signifying scars of unfree existence" (11). David Lloyd, *Representation: The Racial Regime of Aesthetics* (New York: Fordham University Press, 2018).

9 Jacques Rancière, *The Emancipated Spectator*, trans. Gregory Elliott (New York: Verso, 2021), 47, 49.

Carlos Martiel

In a way curiously akin in my perverse mind to what David Lynch does with the Baron, mixing violence and the erotic in complex aesthetic scenes, the Afro-Cuban performance artist Carlos Martiel offers his own body in difficult, even torturous poses or even pierced by objects to prompt—more directly and explicitly—a way of thinking violence and erotics together aesthetically.

He kneels for hours in front of a map of North America. He laboriously upholds a pole. His body is punctured by needles from an American flag. Scars on his body attest to past performances.

Here's art critic Eugenio Viola describing this work at length:

> Martiel . . . aligns his own body—identified with the 'social body'—in ritual-like actions that criticize systems of power and injustice based on race, migration, and isolation. Working in his native Havana and New York City, the artist has constructed a consistent body of work that touches on the very core of the human experience in symbolic reenactments of sorrow, suffering, survival, and privation that are inflected by current events or linked to repressed historical circumstances. [Take *Despojo* (Spoils), 2022 as an example.] In heroic nakedness, the artist stands upright, hands tied in front of him, against a wall painted with the colors of the flag of Chocó, a department that stretches across the northern half of Colombia's Pacific coast. The invocation of Chocó is significant because the Spanish conquistadors built the first cities in South America in this area. After centuries of exploitation, the indigenous communities and people of African descent who inhabit the region continue to struggle with problems of health, education, employment, and civil strife. The dramatically underdeveloped prov-

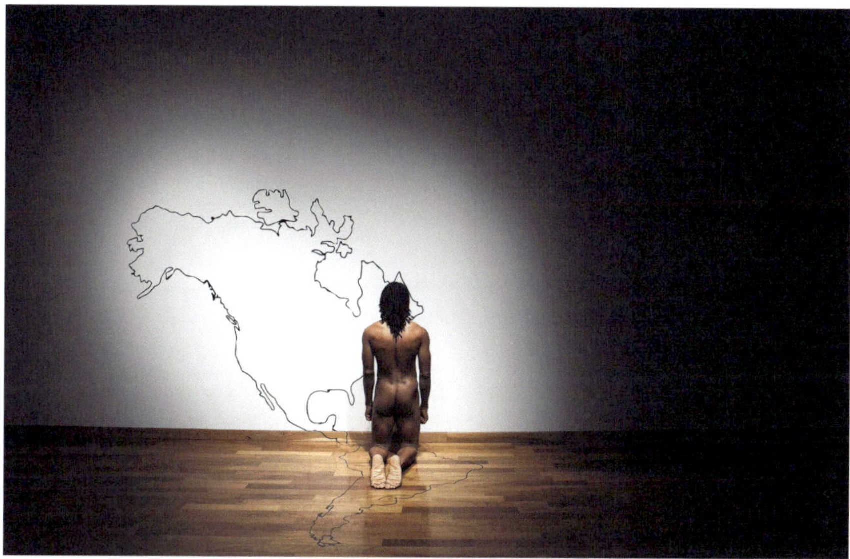

Carlos Martiel, *Encomienda* (2018). Centro Cultural Kirchner (CCK), Buenos Aires, Argentina. Photo by Marcelo Baiardu.

> ince is Colombia's poorest, with one of the country's highest rates of displacement. A construction separating the performance from the public was built from corrugated-zinc sheets riddled with bullet holes, obstructing the view of the artist's body. The public, transformed into accidental voyeurs, could then violate the false privacy of the artist by spying on him through the holes.[1]

Why put oneself through such torturous difficulty? Why spectacularize his body in pain?

There are many ways we can approach such work, such as through the long history of performance art that foregrounds experiences of pain.

Thinking of Chris Burden, Bob Flanagan, Ron Athey, and Catherine Opie, among others, critic Kathy O'Dell writes about the emergence of such work as a way to provoke serious questions about the

---

1 Translated from Italian by Marguerite Shore. Online in *Artforum*: https://www.artforum.com/print/reviews/202303/alexandra-gelis-and-carlos-martiel-90172.

biopolitical disposition of bodies under contemporary regimes of neoliberal capitalism; as she puts it, "We are asked to take responsibility for masochism's institutional causes."[2] Without a doubt, such questioning motivates Martiel's art, demanding that we, as spectators, take account of what happens to beautiful bodies within the many centuries-long savagery—and savagely brutal racism—of capitalist economies.[3]

Take a look at Martiel's performance in New York's Guggenheim Museum, described this way: "On November 10, 2021, with a stern face, immobile, handcuffed, and nude, Martiel stood atop a 50-inch-tall pedestal in the center of the museum's rotunda, temporarily becoming a monument to the historical violence and racism inflicted upon communities of color in the United States."[4]

From the Guggenheim website:

> Martiel first conceived of his *Monumento* series in 2019, with a goal "to become a temporary monument to represent bodies of individuals that historically have been and continue to be discriminated against, oppressed, and excluded by hegemonic Eurocentric and patriarchal discourses." He feels the concept gained heightened resonance in the

---

2 Kathy O'Dell, *Contract with the Skin: Masochism, Performance Art, and the 1970s* (Minneapolis: University of Minnesota Press, 1998), 83–84.

3 In *Sensational Flesh: Race, Power, and Masochism* (New York: NYU Press, 2014), Amber Jamilla Musser writes that, "Whether masochism is connected to colonialism, patriarchy, racialization, or constructions of the self, it relies on a logic that makes sexuality, subjectivity, and agency almost interchangeable terms" (179). An important question arises: how to make the experience of masochism not one of embodied domination, however eroticized as such, but also one of agency, of a different kind of experience of subjectivity?

4 For this and subsequent quotations, see the museum's site: https://www.guggenheim.org/blogs/checklist/the-artist-transforming-himself-into-a-monument-for-the-oppressed. See also Phillipa Snow, who argues in *Which As You Know Means Violence: On Self Injury as Art and Entertainment* (London: Repeater, 2005) that "there is no more extreme material for an artwork than the body, the line between work and artist melting into nothing in a way that suggests either true commitment or insanity depending to the audience's viewpoint" (2).

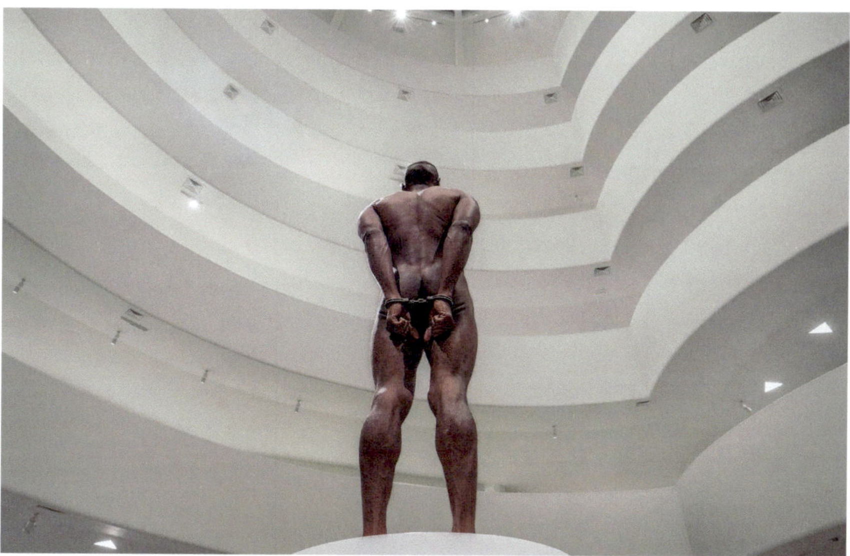

Carlos Martiel, *Monumento II* (2022). Solomon R. Guggenheim Museum, New York. Photo by Enid Alvarez.

> wake of highly publicized examples of violence against Black citizens and communities of color over the past two years.
>
> During *Monumento II*, some visitors observed from the rotunda floor and others from the ramps above, their perspectives changing as they walked up the different levels. Martiel's performance demanded intense concentration and contemplation. Perhaps there was a level of discomfort among museum visitors in viewing a Black man standing nude and handcuffed, using his body as a symbol of oppression to bring to light the fragile lives of Black men in the United States. His presence as a Black male body on a pedestal also signals to the historical perpetuation of the white gaze stemming from the hierarchical structure of power and privilege resulting from colonialism and neoliberalism. Martiel's performative process, in retrospect, is even more unnerving considering how the Black body has been historically subjugated to the pervasiveness of white perception.

The rhetorical situation is crucial here, without a doubt. A Black man standing nude and handcuffed in a museum is itself an important rhetorical interruption of "ordinary affairs," since it underscores the histories of forced labor and racial oppression that undergird the establishment of Western and US wealth, including the accumulation of art and artifacts from across the globe and housed in museums, our palaces designed to showcase the spoils of Western imperialism.[5]

But even more: the fact that Martiel often stages his performances, like *Monumento II*, in major museums of art such as the Guggenheim underscores the ways in which art itself has been used to license and authorize particular forms of *humanity*. David Lloyd: "The terms put in play by aesthetics establish the set of discriminations and distributions by which the Savage comes to be distinguished from the civil subject, the partial and particular human from the universal Subject, and the 'pathological' or suffering, needing, desiring human from the ethical human Subject." Martiel, channeling the "Savage body," confronts the civil subject (note the polite applause if you watch a video of this performance), and, in the rotunda of an iconic museum, he performs the ways in which suffering humans contrast with the evening dress wear of comfortable patrons, calling their own ethicality into question.

Yocari De Los Santos, writing for the Guggenheim website, recorded her reactions to the artist's Guggenheim appearance:

> Martiel's performance provoked in me a wave of different emotions, from a strong feeling of power to one of discomfort and then to a sense of agency—an ability to challenge and deconstruct colonial hegemony. Martiel had a stern, fixed gaze, looking beyond the audience. I wondered about what he was thinking. How does he feel standing immobile on a pedestal? What are his thoughts on the current times we are living, among them, the increase of racial reckoning in museums and across institutions during a global pandemic? What role did the Guggenheim's space play in the execution of "Monumento II"?

5 Note Kimberly Juanita Brown, who writes in *Mortevivum: Photography and the Politics of the Visual* (Cambridge, MA: MIT Press, 2024) that "if documentary 'scenes of subjection' exist devoid of the attendant historical mechanisms of imperial violence, they can appear to illustrate black obsolescence as destiny" (76).

De Los Santos identifies with the artist, imagines feeling his pain standing there, wanting to know what's going on *inside* the artist.

Can I, too, identify? Can I, as a white subject in this culture, *identify* with this Afro-Cuban artist?

How to get at that question . . .

What about the "power of associating and dissociating" that, for Rancière, might disrupt or disturb the range of sensations and excitations that we are culturally conditioned to understand as acceptable, allowable, even legibly human? For sure, when I encounter this work, I experience what De Los Santos experiences, especially the awareness of the critique. I also wonder how Martiel feels standing up there, naked, handcuffed.

Even more complexly, though, I find myself aroused by the beauty of his body and begin to wonder if there's a sexual or erotic dimension to this work that I am interpolated into—and the answer is undoubtedly yes: Part of the horror of subjecting bodies to terror is the excitation of inflicting such damage, and Martiel's work calls powerful attention to the (not always historical) intertwining of violence, power, and the erotic. Though very different, both Lynch's Baron and Martiel's durational performances evoke the intertwining of the sexual and the assertion of hierarchical power, gesturing implicitly—or perhaps explicitly if not fully consciously articulated in Lynch's case—to the circulation of libidinal economies saturating if not indeed structuring political economies.

But there's something else here for me: a collision of the horror of subjection, even abjection, with the libidinal call of a beautiful body—an excess of beauty that, I think, I feel, I hope lies beyond the intertwining of power, violence, and the erotic. Even more, Martiel himself is queer; is he signaling something beyond raw subjection here?

I asked Carlos Martiel if he at all intended his work to be sexually or erotically charged, and he said that he himself does not find the experience of masochistic durational performance at all arousing. I imagine not. But I cannot overlook the fact that, his experience aside, the presence of this well-sculpted and meticulously cared for body offers an aesthetic experience that, at the very least, *contrasts* with the torturous bondage through which it is being placed, the two dimensions throwing one another into sharp relief.

How do I account for my reactions, my erotic feeling for this performance piece? Can I account for them outside, or to the side, of the intertwining of the erotic, violence, and power? My challenge is not to deny the erotic in the exercise of power, but maybe to read and experience it *queerly*, just as I experienced Lynch's Baron queerly.[6]

I won't stop myself from saying that what I can do is desire this body, this body put on display. And I do desire it. I want to touch it. I want to care for it. I want to uncuff the hands and move my own hands up and down this body in comfort.

Not everyone will experience these things, for sure, and such desires are likely far beyond the artist's intention of presenting his body in distress in the halls of beauty. But the juxtaposition of horror with the space of the museum is itself juxtaposed by the beauty of the body. And what is important to me in witnessing this work is what was important to me in sitting down in a movie theater in 1984 and seeing the Baron delight in his queerness. No, I do not sadomasochistically delight in the pain of this body, but I cannot deny my desire for it.

6 Jacques Rancière might help us understand why such reactions, this erotic aesthetics over and beyond the rhetorics of the performance, are important, even crucial, to the experience of this kind of work. He argues that "what is common is 'sensation.' Human beings are tied together by a certain sensory fabric, a certain distribution of the sensible, which defines their way of being together; and politics is about the transformation of the sensory fabric of 'being together.' . . . The solitude of the artwork is a false solitude: it is an intertwining or twisting together of sensations, like the cry of a human body. And a human collective is an intertwining and twisting together of sensations in the same way" (56). Martiel, perhaps, may be asking that we identify and adopt his attitude, but what happens for some of us is a bit different. I may attempt rhetorically to adopt his attitude about the problem of the oppression of Black bodies in the name of the maintenance of certain kinds of white supremacist civilization. But this is also, for many of us, a false identification in many senses; many of us cannot *identify* with his racial positioning in our culture. I, for one, cannot—even as robust as I imagine my imagination to be. Jacques Rancière, *The Emancipated Spectator*, trans. Gregory Elliott (New York: Verso, 2021).

But there is danger here. Martiel presenting his body for viewing in the Guggenheim rotunda as a recalling of histories of the slave trade and the trafficking of Black bodies is also enacting the spectacle of the Black body in display for consumption in the *here and now*. In witnessing and then even describing this work, am I consuming this body? Am I trying to capture it myself, make it do my own aesthetic and political work? Can I escape the circuits of power—and power vectored through eroticized aesthetics—that seems always to position Black bodies as sites of capture and consumption?

And what kind of consumption? Martiel, naked and handcuffed, offers not just the spectacle of a beautiful body but a body in *distress*.[7]

The danger here, the danger *I* face in writing about Martiel, is that of a white man presenting a Black body for spectacular viewing. This is nothing new. Whites have been photographing and talking about Black bodies since the invention of photography. Even "admiring" photographers—think Mapplethorpe—can't escape the fundamental problem of a white person presenting a Black body for capture and then consumption by others, usually white.[8] How do I avoid stereotypes? How do I resist the desire of limiting the representation—and thus the understanding—of Black experience? Maybe Barthes was

7 Jafari S. Allen notes the many ways in which white spectators, albeit with good intentions, capture the Black body and limit it by turning attention again and again to that body as always in danger, in peril, in distress. He writes to his readers in *There's a Disco Ball Between Us: A Theory of Black Gay Life* (Durham, NC: Duke University Press, 2021) that this kind of capture, this aesthetic approach, is woefully insufficient, even dangerous: "But dear reader, you likely want to hear about how imperiled and sick(ened) we are, or how always already dead we are. Perhaps you are convinced that there is no we at all: simply a nothing. With nothing between us" (xi). Allen's is a book about desire, about Black desire, about trying to think *beyond* pain: "I want us to see and say and keep safe something that re-members, incites, helps, and heals. Therefore, this is also a kind of love letter" (198).

8 In *We Were Here: Sexuality, Photography, and Cultural Difference: Selected Writings by Sunil Gupta*. (New York: Aperture, 2022) Sunil Gupta writes about this problem *within queer communities specifically* in "Desire and Black Men," noting that "Every conceivable kind of gay male sex [including Black bodies] has been photographed; the debate around representation within the gay movement has revolved around the need to stimulate desire and the desirability of limiting sexual role models to just a few stereotypes" (25).

right, wandering through that New York porn shop: The images of bodies in bondage can only incite a repetition of the image, distancing one from the realness of the experience. How much more significant must that be for white consumers of Black bodies in bondage.

I want to position my approach to Martiel's work—to Martiel's Black body—*precisely within this context*. Martiel himself has already offered his body in the rotunda of the Guggenheim; he is already staging for us the confrontation between Black bodies and white consumption. I am trying to acknowledge that that is what he is doing, and then—further—interrogate within myself the flow of different desires, the flow from a sadomasochistic twitching to the desire to touch and comfort. That is, I'm not trying to position *his* work or *his* body, but *my* approach to it.

Some are going to suggest that such a separation is not possible. I'm going to suggest that it might not be possible, but that the failure to *attempt* it keeps us all locked into modes of subjection that limit the capacities of desire to allow us to think, feel, and be differently—that might limit our capacities to touch, to comfort.

Maybe.

I am insisting that this kind of aesthetic response might be absolutely necessary in some cases to understand the function of how we move in and through the world and through and with other bodies. Put another way, the political economy that Martiel's work demands we account for (the building of our culture on the backs of Black bodies) cannot be disentangled from the libidinal economies that put our culture's desires for domination into play in the first place. Even more, recognition of those same libidinal economies might allow us better critical insight into how desires for domination motivate political economies.

And even further, I'm hoping, a particular kind of *queer* response to this particular body might open up space for a whole other ethic of care, or play, or pleasure, or possibility.[9]

9 Again, in *The Emancipated Spectator*, Rancière says that the aesthetic experience "is a multiplication of connections and disconnections that reframe the relation between bodies, the world they live in and the way in which they are 'equipped' to

To find a way to care, to care for this body. To care for one another.

My care, my desire find refraction in Martiel's own care for his body, a care suffused with ethical considerations. When I asked, Martiel reported that "I have an exercise routine of 5 days per week, but when I am traveling it's difficult for me to follow it so I do walks of 1 hour daily. Besides being vegan and a whole food plant base with no consumption of processed food, even if they are vegan products. My diet is salt, sugar and oil free." This ethic of bodily care manifests in the aesthetic beauty of a body put on display—a body that articulates its own power to attract, to intrigue, to excite.

To critique, certainly. Without a doubt. But also to attract.

What I am arguing for here might not pertain to all art. But I do think it pertains to a certain kind of critical art, a certain kind of queer critical art. At the same time, what I am arguing for here is hardly limited to the aesthetic receptivity of queer people, even as I do think it pertains to our current moment of cultural production in which, lacking concrete plans of action for directions that will lead to amelioration of inequities or the creation of more just human relationships, we need at the very least a *feeling*, a *felt sense* of beauty as powerful—an aesthetic appreciation, however inarticulate at times, that is more than just the recognition of a shared capacity and that animates a desire not just to connect but to change the conditions of what is possible and desirable.[10]

---

adapt to it. It is a multiplicity of folds and gaps in the fabric of common experience that change the cartography of the perceptible, the thinkable and the feasible. As such, it allows for new modes of political construction of common objects and new possibilities of collective enunciation" (72). Martiel would likely agree; he likely wants the presence of his naked and handcuffed body in the middle of the Guggenheim Museum to "change the cartography of the perceptible, the thinkable and the feasible" in the wider world. But one way it does that—a way that he himself doesn't account for—is through the eyes and senses of at least one queer person who sees the vulnerability of the body as an opening to care, as the possibility of a different kind of coming together.

10 David Lloyd, in *Under Representation: The Racial Regime of Aesthetics* (New York: Fordham University Press, 2018), could be talking about the experience of seeing Carlos Martiel queerly when he writes, "Even 'damaged life' . . . imagines

Damaged life. But also enjoyment, even possibly creation.

My interest here is in keeping responses to work like Martiel's robust, odd, unusual, queer. A flattened approach would extend sympathy to bruised and damaged bodies. Such seems not irrelevant but frankly insufficient given the drastic nature of the racial, sexual, and ecological crises facing us.

Such an aesthetics requires work. The identification with the Baron offered in Lynch's film is not one of queer worldbuilding but rather of queer pathologization. I had to access a different, more sensory dimension of experience to do something different with what I was being offered, to turn it into something that was more affirming than damaging. In a different way with Martiel's work, I recognize on the one hand the rhetorical power of the connections he is making, the intervention of suffering Black bodies into the pristine spaces of the museum, the request to identify with that suffering, at least, as a sympathetic gesture of acknowledging the ongoing impact of racism and the building of our culture on white supremacy. On the other hand, I also sense possibilities for feeling and responding in ways even more powerfully evocative and potentially grounding for a different kind of ethic and relationality—an ethic of intimate, even erotic care.

What does such care make possible? What does desire make possible? How does a failure to attend to our desires make opaque the possibilities of living differently, being otherwise with ourselves and one another? What do we miss when we do not think about what we *want* more acutely, more carefully, more ethically? What damages do we perpetuate when we fail to want more, more actually, more carefully, more ethically?[11]

---

forms of living that are not merely reactive but rather discover new forms of resistance and enjoyment, of survival and creation" (17–18). Lloyd goes on to say: "But whatever those spaces may eventually allow, the return of the aesthetic to the feeling, desiring, even the fearing, pathological subject continues to offer the prospect of a living otherwise in the face of the generalized state of exception with which the neoliberal state has displaced the 'unilateral declaration of universality' of the liberal racial order" (18).

11 A related question arises for me: Is there a queer critical and affective pedagogy here? One that intertwines both political and aesthetic experiences not just to experience more astutely and deeply the experience of power but also to experience

What do we want?

What *do* we want?

I'm wandering about the Menil Museum in Houston, a place close to where I grew up, New Orleans. I'm a guest of a university, in the prime of my life, my career. I tell myself all the time that my life is perfect, even when it isn't. I'm here, now, enjoying this art—my academic position, at least, if not my sense of myself, established, secure.

I see a young man, tall, built, carefully studying a painting. He's wearing a wife-beater, black, but skimpy enough that I see a large tattoo, black, spanning his upper back.

PAIN IS TRUTH

It's so fucking beautiful. I can't look at the picture he's looking at, I don't remember what he was looking at, so intent am I at holding my gaze on his back as he intently examines the image in front of him. I lift my phone to take an image. I want to approach him and ask him about his tattoo. It's huge. I know it must have hurt like a motherfucker. But it's beautiful, so fucking beautiful, like this young man, this beautiful young man whose beauty is in part the intensity of his attention, focused on the image in front of him.

---

in it the potential for a different libidinal exchange? A reeducation of desire, that is? Pushing on this, what happens if we challenge the current distribution of the sensible enough to allow for other kinds of feelings and responses beyond identification? The distribution of the sensible has changed enough to allow more and varied kinds of bodies into its spaces. But is that enough? No, I believe. Rather, what I think is called for now more than ever is a pedagogy of affective and erotic reflection, one will ask all of us to think and feel through the sensibilities we bring with us and then challenge us to expand those sensibilities to extend ourselves to one another in gestures of care and possibility. Attending to desire, and its potential reeducation, is hardly a panacea. Redistributing the possibilities for the sensible can only be one strategy among many we need to try to refashion our world and our relationship to it—our damaged world, our damaged relations, our damaged bodies. I'm convinced that we will not live by argument alone but rather by attending more astutely to what we want and how we might work together to fashion a world that can maximize responsible attention to fulfilling our needs and desires in the most cooperative and sustainable ways possible.

I don't approach him. But I keep his image, the image of his intensity, the image of my own intensity in beholding him, the brief communion he'll never know.

Pain is truth.

I remember an old poet: "Beauty is Truth, Truth Beauty."

The boy is beautiful, his tattoo, beautiful.

But what truth do we want?

What truth can we actually stand, about ourselves, about others, about the damages we've endured, the damages we've inflicted, the damages we've inflicted on ourselves?

Catherine Opie

I can't *not* think of Catherine Opie when I think about blood, queerness, extremity, damage. When I think about Laura Aguilar, her beautiful round body that she would cut because of the pain inside, I think of Opie. When I think of Carlos Martiel standing handcuffed in the rotunda of the Guggenheim Museum, willfully submitting to torture to make a point about the painful legacies of how our culture treats Black bodies, I also think of Opie. When I think of Guibert and Morrisroe, dying of AIDS, their blood contaminated with a disease, an infection, that governments at the time didn't want to treat because it was helping eliminate some of the "undesirables," I think too of Opie.

Opie makes pictures that resonate with all of these artists, sometimes overtly, sometimes implicitly. To be sure, she's not the same. The differences matter. As, too, the resonances.

I'm thinking in particular of *Self Portrait/Cutting*.

What's going on in 1993? In the world? In my life?

Clinton had just been elected, bringing to a close twelve years of Republican rule, of trickle-down bullshit and wars waged to fill the coffers of oil men. Some ground is made on treating HIV, but thousands and thousands still die. It will be years before more effective treatments make living with HIV a real possibility.

In more general news for queer folks, even a Democratic president, while sympathetic in ways that Reagan's inhumanity wouldn't allow, even Clinton can't quite bring himself to grant full civil rights to queer people, even if he does eventually get "Don't Ask, Don't Tell" passed, allowing queer people to serve in the military—in the

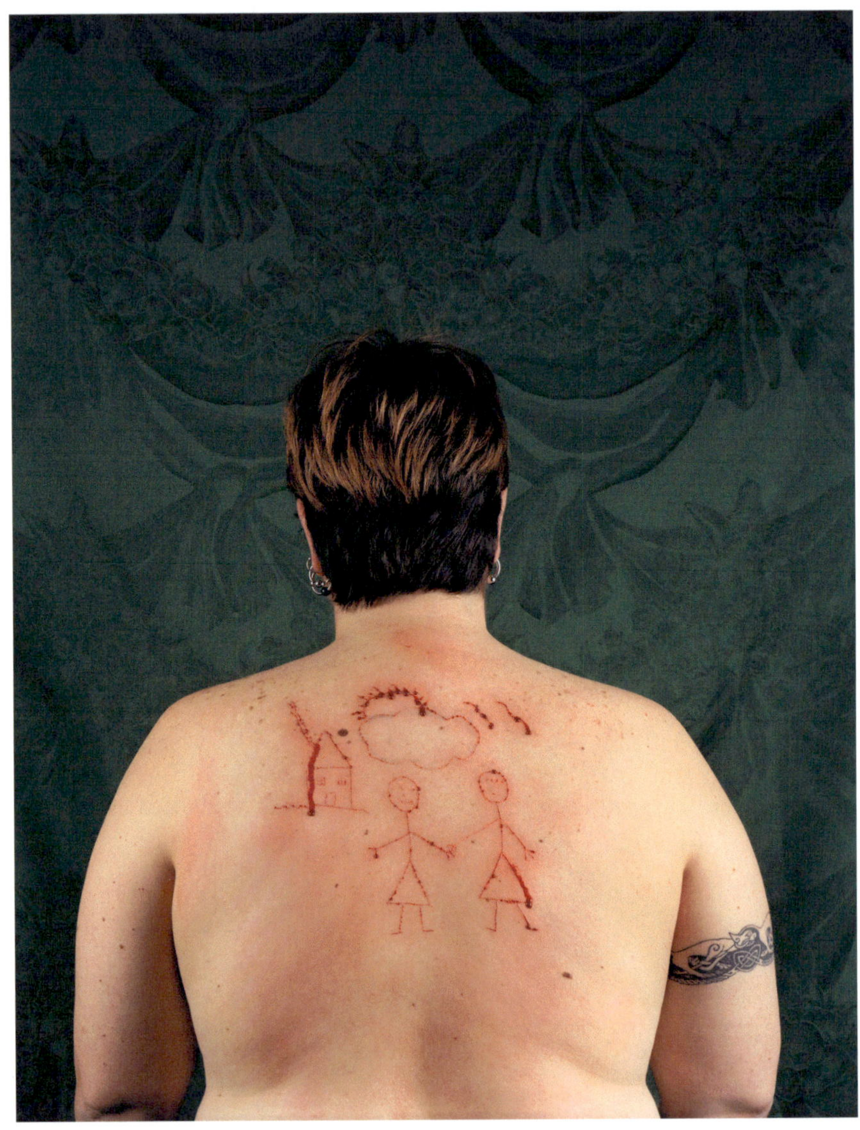

Catherine Opie, *Self-Portrait/Cutting* (1993). © Catherine Opie, Courtesy Regen Projects, Los Angeles, Lehmann Maupin, New York, Hong Kong, London, and Seoul, and Thomas Dane Gallery, London and Naples.

military!—if they keep their mouths shut. Despite this half-assed attempt to protect queer people in the military, thousands and thousands of people are still kicked out, with people of color and women disproportionately affected.

Personally, I had just finished my PhD in comparative literature and got married to a woman with whom I was in love. We headed to Colorado together, leaving Louisiana behind, to make a new life for ourselves, hopefully among people who would be a bit more sympathetic to our progressive views.

I read that sentence again and again, and I think about how marrying a woman—even a woman I was in love with—was the only way I could imagine getting out of Louisiana, out of a homophobic culture, even if just to a slightly less homophobic culture. And while I won't tell her story, I believe that we both needed each other: We needed to help each other get out, move on, rebuild ourselves, and a life, somewhere else.

Getting married. Making family. The only way we could imagine to correct or *counter* the damages done.

But family? What kind of family? I knew I'd never have children. She didn't want them either. And I didn't deceive her about myself. She knew about my crushes on guys. She knew I was at least bisexual, or biromantic. We talked endlessly, it seems, about my need for a "male friend," something I couldn't quite find in my religiously conservative communities. It all seems so very D. H. Lawrence, in retrospect. But it's where I was, where we were.

Married. Making family. Even if only with each other.

Catherine Opie *could* imagine, here in California, having spent so much time documenting the lives of queers, leather queers, queer subcultures—she could imagine other kinds of family, the kinds of family that, just a couple of years after we got married and moved to Colorado, I started imagining, going to bisexual support groups, forming friendships with queer people, eventually my wife and I divorcing but remaining friends because that was the greatest way we could love one another, to love one another enough to let each other go so we could explore and pursue the kinds of lives and relationships and communities that would make us happy, or at least make happiness possible—divorce because we couldn't quite imagine together an open relationship, polyamory, an expanding circle of friends and lovers *together*. The possibility flickered at the edges of my mind, but just so, just a flicker, not a light.

I hadn't yet seen Opie's photographs. Oh, for sure, I knew queers existed. I spent a chunk of 1995 poring over Marjorie Garber's *Vice Versa*, a veritable treasure trove documenting and exploring bisexual images, texts, films, plays, artists, creators.[1] I read many books about queer people, *by* queer people. I took a copy of James Baldwin's *Another Country* on our honeymoon. I *knew*. But I didn't. You can read and read and read, but that's not knowing. As much as I love reading, value the time spent exploring and learning, it isn't knowing. It isn't knowing in your bones that something is possible.

So I hadn't seen Opie's photographs, but if I had, would they have changed my life? I'm not sure. I'm never sure about any of this, about the power of art, of writing, of creating to change things. As soon as I write that, I know I'm wrong. Art *does* change lives. But the change is never simple, rarely direct, often complicated and full of strange and unexpected twists and turns. It builds over time. It amasses. The change is subtle, until it's not.

Seeing Opie's picture, the one I just showed you, would've been one more aesthetic experience added to a trove of experiences of documented queerness that I had been collecting, building, archiving. When I finally came out, I could speak *volumes* about being queer, even if my actual experience of queerness was limited. Art *did* change me. And other people's writing about queerness changed me. But it wasn't, for me at least, a conversion, a sudden transformation, but more a careful sedimenting, layering, accretion, so that, when I *was* ready, I had not only a language but a way of imagining the life I wanted. When I was ready to *know*, I already, in my own way, *knew*.

1 Marjorie Garber, *Vice Versa: Bisexuality and the Eroticism of Everyday Life* (New York: Simon & Schuster, 1996).

Now, though—now, I have *so much* I could say about Opie's photograph, so much to say because it provides me, well over three decades into my openly lived queerness, a way not just to imagine queerness but to meditate on it, to probe it, even to pick at its scabs. Because yes, there are scabs. There is damage, damage accrued, amassed, endured, survived. I've been telling you about it, about the damage, the scabs.

Opie's back, pierced, cut, wounded. I can't imagine that those cuts didn't scab over. What do they look like now? Is the outline of the house, the women, still visible? Or has it faded in the intervening decades? Does she ever retrace those cuts with a blade, allowing the wounded flesh to form more lasting, visible scars, a puckering of damaged flesh?

Would she, the artist, the photographer, like my use of the words "damage" and "wound" to describe what she's done to herself? I resist the urge to ask her, even though we have had some limited correspondence. But I resist. I don't ask her. I want to wonder because the wondering, the questioning, allows me to approach some of my own more difficult questions, some of my own more challenging damages and wounds, even if Opie might not think of the cuts and her photograph in the same language, with the same words.

Damage. *Wound.*

I'm not the only one thinking of this photograph, the only one trying to choose their words carefully to describe what the photograph represents, what it speaks to.

Here's Deborah Bright: "Opie's . . . photograph is a self-portrait with a stick-figure drawing of two girls holding hands in front of a house, cut into the broad expanse of the photographer's emphatically butch back. The primal wish for the family harmony this drawing so economically maps materializes in the rich red life-blood of the artist who also alludes to a ritualized practice of s/m."[2]

---

2 Deborah Bright, *The Passionate Camera: Photography and Bodies of Desire* (New York: Routledge, 1998), 145.

Bright touches on Opie's connection to the leather community, and that's there, for sure. Ritualized cutting is a part of that community, not practiced by all, but by some, like piercing and branding as well. I imagine that cutting might be, in today's parlance, a bit too triggering for some, perhaps for those whose cutting stems from an overwhelming pain or self-hatred, self-disgust. But maybe even for those "pathological" cutters, cutting in the context of s/m might be . . . healing? I don't know. I don't know if this is what Opie herself is doing. Again, I haven't inquired. It's more interesting for me to wonder, and then to read Deborah Bright's reading of the photograph and think, *Oh my, how positive, how positively positive this reading is.* How full and robust, even at the level of language: the "broad expanse," the "emphatically butch back," the "primal wish," the "family harmony," the "rich red life-blood." Bright is emphatic, even ecstatic about this photo. It is a photo *of ecstasy*, of a primal wish for family harmony that has beautifully, if childlike, seared itself into the great back flesh of this robust person.

Bright is not the only critic who wants to . . . *save?* . . . this photograph from being misunderstood as one about damage, about being wounded. And I get that. Queers have had enough damage, enough woundedness. But the leaps and twists toward positivity themselves accrue in ways that demand their own accounting. I'm thinking of Maggie Nelson and her wonderful book, *The Art of Cruelty*, in which the poet/critic writes stunningly about artists who seem to torture themselves, and sometimes others, in various aesthetic pursuits.[3] Think of Chris Burden shooting himself, or crawling on his stomach, with his hands bound behind his back, over shards of glass. Nelson doesn't write, as I recall, specifically in this book about *Self-Portrait/Cutting*, but she *does* consider a neighboring

3 Maggie Nelson, *The Art of Cruelty* (New York: W. W. Norton, 2012). Nelson describes her overarching project this way: "the aim is to attend closely to the different excitements and effects of this 'pure cruelty' (such as precision, transgression, purgation, productive unease, abjectness, radical exposure, uncanniness, unnerving frankness, acknowledged sadism and masochism, a sense of clearing or clarity), while also staying keenly attuned to the various sophistries and self-justifications that so often attend its valorization" (6).

piece, *Self-Portrait/Pervert* from 1994, and how she talks about it resonates with Bright's positive depiction of *Cutting*. Moving on from a discussion of some truly cruel artwork, pieces that explore human cruelty to others and to self, Nelson practically catches her breath when writing about Opie:

> What a relief . . . to shift one's attention to an image such as *Self-Portrait/Pervert*, the iconic 1994 self-portrait by photographer Catherine Opie. In *Pervert*, Opie is formally seated, facing the camera, her hands crossed in her lap, an ornate tapestry hanging behind her. A glossy black leather S/M hood encases her face; forty-six needles have been ritually inserted up and down her tattooed arms; and the word "Pervert" has been freshly carved, in ornate lettering, into the skin of her chest. Her body squarely presents itself to us as bleeding, resilient, imperial, and desirous . . .

How can I not love the adjectives and adverbs here? Formally, ornate, ritually, freshly, ornate (again!), resilient, imperial, desirous. The ecstatic world of s/m is once again before us, the power and pleasure of an admittedly extreme practice is rendered in Nelson's prose as a formally rich and complex presentation of Opie's artistic ascendance; she is "resilient, imperial, and desirous."

Nelson goes on:

> *Pervert* is decidedly uninterested in what others might do to a passive female body. Opie's self-portrait speaks to the opposite: it broadcasts what Opie's body likes, what it wants—indeed, what it is: a pervert, stated brightly in flesh and blood. Its solidity, its composure, its reclamatory *Pervert* announcement, all say, The buck stops here. The meticulousness of the cutting and the needle-work signifies intent, resiliency, and training; likewise, the mask indicates a gratified [*sic*] desire for effacement rather than a silencing. Opie bleeds when punctured, as do we all. But her bloodshed here signifies solidarity—a shared kinship with the queer leather community from which much of Opie's early work emanates, as well as with the work of gay male artists (such as Ron Athey, Opie's friend, subject, and collaborator), for whom the public shedding of blood—especially HIV-positive blood—during the

> height of the AIDS epidemic was experienced as an act of catharsis and defiance. Such a stance rejects the burden of abjected precariousness; as a result, the whiff of cruelty is nowhere to be found.[4]

Much of the force of Nelson's analysis here is in picturing Opie's photograph as a picture not just of the photographer's resilience but of her disregard for "what others might do to a passive female body." The image is all about agency, agency, agency. She is not silenced, but "gratified" in the choices she is making about her own body. Nelson situates this photograph and Opie's work alongside that of Ron Athey, whose work offers an even more extreme (or should I say "daring" to keep the tone here positive?) exploration of how the body can be made to speak beyond—and in frank defiance—of abjection, precariousness, and cruelty.

As Nelson says, "the whiff of cruelty is nowhere to be found."

I don't want to say outright that Nelson is wrong, if only because I think that she's making and marking an important intervention in queer pain, an intervention in the long twentieth-century history of queer abjection and damage. In this guise, she's all too right on target, and her insights about Opie, and even Athey, have not just a certain merit, but a delightful vigor and force.

But saying there's not even a "whiff of cruelty" just doesn't seem right to me. I mean, c'mon: not even a *whiff*?

Maybe the whiff I'm catching is the stale odor of some of my own damage, my own woundedness, especially when I get to the lines in Nelson's argument about "blood-letting" as a kind of catharsis and defiance in the wake of so much talk, so much politically generated and frankly hateful talk, about queers being so pathological that, of course, their blood would be contaminated too, their social contagion made materially manifest in the spread of HIV.

I can't help but think of my first HIV test, in the early 1990s, likely around the time when Opie was conceiving of her photograph. I was about to get married and wanted to make sure I was "clean" before we consummated

4 Ibid., 198–99.

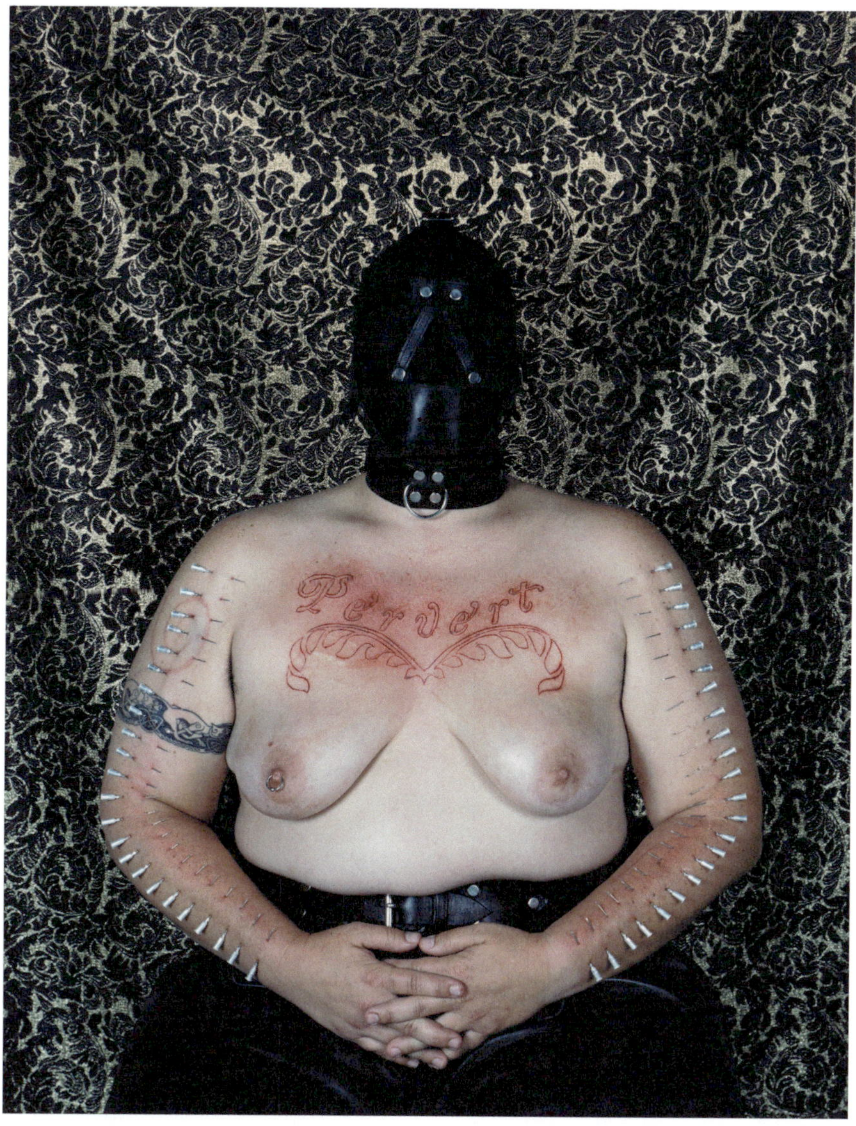

Catherine Opie, *Self-Portrait /Pervert* (1994). © Catherine Opie, Courtesy Regen Projects, Los Angeles, Lehmann Maupin, New York, Hong Kong, London, and Seoul, and Thomas Dane Gallery, London and Naples.

our marriage. I'd fooled around with a guy in college, and I didn't think that I was infected, but I wasn't going to risk it.

I stopped by the student health center on campus and asked for the test. I was silently led back to the nurse's station, where a middle-aged white woman drew the blood for the test. She barely spoke to me, frowning the entire time. I didn't think much of her demeanor until another nurse walked by and asked her what I was in for.

"That HIV test."

"What a shame," the other nurse replied, both of them frowning and shaking their heads.

These women, both white and middle-aged, had no idea why I was getting the test, no idea that I had fooled around with a guy, no idea that I was struggling (as we said at the time) with my sexuality. But the stigma around HIV and AIDS was so great that even just asking for the test was enough to evoke not just pity but scorn.

When I called two weeks later to get the test results—can you believe that? I had to wait two weeks to get results, such were the protocols at the time—the nurse who answered my call asked what I was calling for. I told her, and I heard her rustling through papers. She then came back on the line and said, "I'll have to get a doctor to talk to you."

I stopped breathing. I couldn't breathe. Why would a doctor have to talk to me unless the news was the worst possible? I couldn't breathe.

After a minute, the doctor came on the line and told me that I was fine, all negative. Apparently, at that time in Louisiana, only a doctor could deliver test results for HIV. I wondered: Why didn't the nurse tell me that? What agony could she have spared me? But no, I'm sure she didn't tell me so she could punish me, could make me wait a bit longer to get the results, could make me squirm with fear, could put the fear of the lord in me for even having had to take the test in the first place.

I'll never forget this. I'll never forget the subtle cruelty—yes, Maggie, there's some cruelty for you—the cruelty with which I was handled. And I wasn't even announcing my queerness. Just that little bit of proximity to HIV, AIDS, the diseased, the queer—that was enough in 1992, 1993, in Louisiana, in the Deep South, in the United States of America, to warrant scornful cruelty.

My blood did not carry HIV. But it might as well have, given that I had to ask for the test in the first place, even if just to prevent my transmission of the virus to someone else.

I wanted to protect whatever family my wife and I were going to have, but proximity to queerness was already showing me how difficult that was going to be. Still, we persisted. We married and moved on, and then we split when we needed to.

If I had seen Opie's picture in 1993, 1994, I wonder what I would've thought about her depiction of family. I wonder what I would've felt.

I suspect I would have marveled at the sheer audacity of having carved into her back an image of lesbian love, of two women, holding hands, making house. I was soon to read in the 1990s about how Michel Foucault believed that it wasn't the specter of two men fucking that disturbed people but the idea that those two men would wake up and decide to love one another, to set up house together. Surely the same, or a version, of that disturbance would accrue around two women waking up and deciding to make a home, a life, together. I didn't need Foucault to tell me that in the early '90s. I knew it, deeply, profoundly. That was going to be the problem. Hence it was easier to marry a woman and see what we could do, what kind of expansive life we could make, than to try to be queer in the Deep South. I knew by 1996, when marrying a woman didn't work out, that I was going to have to figure out how to make a life, make a *home*, with someone like me, a man, a lover, with whom I would hope one day to wake and decide to set up house together.

I did. I *did* wake up with a boy and decide to make a home, and by 1997, 1998, we were on our way.

But the image, even then, Opie's image, would've seemed fantastical, like a daring, a bravery, a courage. A defiance, as the critics say. It would have seemed—and it *did* seem—like something carved into my back. Like a mark. Like a *cut* into my flesh. Like a wound.

It *was* a wound. It *was* a wound, deciding to wake up with a boy in my bed and set up house together. It was a wound in the '90s, even in Clinton's somewhat more tolerant America. It was a wound. I'm sorry, Maggie, I'm really sorry, but I was a wound. Not just defiant.

I know that's not popular to say. I know that. But I have to say it anyway, even though the critics want to talk about our defiance, our queer defiance. Sure, it *was* defiant. But it *hurt*. Badly. I remember talking to my mother on the phone in 1997, wanting to, *trying* to talk to her about Mack, the boy in my life, and her dreadful, honest response: "Don't tell me about the evil in your life. We don't love you for who you are. We love you for the person we know you could be."

I hung up the phone and didn't talk to her for a while. That was my defiance. But fuck anyone who doesn't understand that that was also a wound, that her words *cut* into me, deeply, lastingly. I can't talk about my defiance without talking about *cruelty*. And even though my mother and I would eventually reconcile and find a way to love one another again—love one another for who we are, not just who we imagine each other to be, or even *want* each other to be—even though we would love again, the words left a cut, a mark.

A wound. A bit of damage.

I sit with my husband, the former evil in my life, and my mother—I sit with both of them for dinner in our home, the home the three of us now share, and I am glad. I have joy, even, at times.

And I also have a wound. A cut.

I will always have that cut.

So I understand Opie's picture, her photograph of her cut back, as robustly broad and butch as it is, as a complex statement about family. About the wounds of family. About the wounds of family that have denied us, that have forced us to be defiant—defiant that is, when they haven't succeeded in killing us—even though they *have* killed so many of us. Family has been toxic for so many, many queer and trans people.[5]

---

5 Lauri Firstenberg calls Opie's *Self Portrait* an anti-portrait, one that "unrelentingly refutes contact with the photographic gaze" and that also "attempts a play between photographically obscuring queer identity and asserting the stereotype through concrete signs and bodily marks of 'butch' haircut and tattooing" (317). Firstenberg, "Autonomy and the Archive in America: Reexamining the Intersec-

And then there are the wounds of building a family, even a queer family, even a family that you choose. Because, well, it's difficult. Any family is difficult. Any intimacy is difficult. But also because our world continues to *make* it difficult for queers and trans folk. Building our worlds, building our lives together—this lovemaking, this homemaking, is built on wounds and is itself an invitation to wound, to cut, to endure the damage.[6]

To endure.

To find joy? Yes. Joy and solace and comfort and love.

But it cuts too.

It cuts.

I can't write any of these words and not wonder if I'm suggesting a kind of *ontology* of queerness or arguing about damage as somehow necessary to the queer experience. I don't want to believe that, and I don't want that for future generations of queers and trans people. But I won't pull punches and deny that it has been a profound part of my own experience. Damage. The wound, the many wounds.

The cut.

But ontological? I'm not sure. I'm not sure in part because I resist ontologies in general. I don't think there's anything like a gene or a psychodynamic that *makes* one queer. I have held, theoretically, with other queer theorists that queerness is always positional, in relation to social norms and cultural strictures and political realities—and the need to resist such.

But my writing here suggests that, while queer may be positional, my queerness has also been *experiential*, experiential in ways that call attention to larger structures that position me, that mark me, that cut

---

tion of Photography and Stereotype," in *Only Skin Deep: Changing Visions of the American Self*, ed. Coco Fusco and Brian Wallis (New York: International Center of Photography/Abrams, 2003).

6 In *Contract With the Skin: Masochism, Performance Art, and the 1970s* (Minneapolis: University of Minnesota Press, 1998) Kathy O'Dell notes about *Self Portrait* that "approval must be constructed within oneself. In the context of rampant homophobia, this self-construction process can be painful, as each razor cut in Opie's back seems to suggest" (80).

me. I've never been able to "hide" my queerness for long. And not just because I'm willful, defiant even. But because I'm a bit effeminate for a man, a bit unusual in my mannerisms, a bit . . . *queer*. Always have been, from a very very young age. Fag, faggot, queer, sissy—these were all words from my *early childhood. Early childhood.* How does a near lifetime of hearing such words, enduring homophobic bullying, experiencing exclusion from family bonds because of my queerness—how do we live through a world in which queerness is constantly a site of legal battle and contestation, in which I've been in one voting booth after another facing levers about whether or not I and my kind *deserved* equal rights, civil rights, access to social and political goods and enfranchisement—how can any of that *experience*, lived over *decades and decades*, not in some way be formative, be *foundational* for who I am?

How can any of that not constitute a sustained attack, an attack that leaves me at least partially damaged, partially *formed* through a constant barrage of *insult*? It may not, ultimately, be ontological. But it is crucial to my understanding of myself.

As I near the end of this book, I want to pause over my last comment, because I recognize that it builds on both a longstanding debate about queerness in our culture—what are its origins, its ontology?—and a counter movement that understands queerness as created and experienced within sociocultural and political structures. And is there anything that's simultaneously more intimately personal and profoundly social than the experience of insult? Being insulted, a form of damage, a cut into the self, is experienced as a deeply personal assault, but it always comes from an interaction, from people who have weighed you and found you wanting, from a structure that judges.

That cuts.

I take the word "insult" from the work of someone I've already mentioned in passing, Didier Eribon, whose book *Insult and the Making of the Gay Self* offers carefully considered reflections on the issue of gay subjectivity, on the possibility of identifying a common thread in what it means to be "gay" (the word he uses, writing in the 1990s and publishing his book in 2000). Drawing on the work of Foucault, whose first major biography was written by Eribon, the author examines the proposition that there is no basis upon which to assert a commonality of gay experience or identity. While dismissing congenital and biological "origins," Eribon *does* argue, though, that *enduring insult* may be the single most common experience of gay people: "All of the studies done in homosexual populations (of either sex) show that the experience of insult (not to mention of physical violence) is one of the most widely shared elements of their existence." He presents his central argument more fully in the following passage:

> Is not the whole life of gay people entirely defined by permanent "moral harassment," be it direct or indirect, a harassment present in every situation in which they find themselves, a social harassment? And are not the personalities that they construct and the identities that they shape determined by the psychological consequences of the "harassed" social position they occupy in daily life (produced by ambient insults, mockery, aggression, hostility)? It is not hard to understand why one of the structuring principles of gay and lesbian subjectivities consists in seeking out means to flee insult and violence, whether it be by way of dissimulation or by way of emigration to more hospitable locations.[7]

This is a profound and provocative view, and, in chapter after chapter and example after example, Eribon demonstrates that insult—bearing the brunt of "mockery, aggression, hostility"—is a common enough experience of many gays to warrant insult as a foundational component of gay subjectivity. Drawing on his own experience, scholarly research, and the works of Proust, Gide, Wilde, and Foucault, Eribon traces how homophobic insult has shaped the personality and psyche of gays for the past hundred-plus years.

To be clear: It is not that we are *born* damaged, but that we are born *into* a world that often seeks to damage us with its homophobic attacks. From the experience of keeping one's sexual interests

7 Didier Eribon, *Insult and the Making of the Gay Self*, trans. Michael Lucey (Durham, NC: Duke University Press, 2004), 18–19.

closeted, to feelings of paranoia, to the necessity of leading double lives, to even more recent attempts to gain legitimacy through civil rights legislation and political recognition—Eribon sees all of these as fundamentally motivated by a people who have been subject to harassment and insult—subject to damage.

Eribon's goal in writing *Insult* is, ultimately, not necessarily to counter poststructuralist claims that gay identity, like *all* identity, is without essential substance, but to assert that gays have a fundamental commonality of experience that begs for consideration—and justice. Eve Kosofsky Sedgwick, one of the founders of the academic discipline known as queer theory, might call this a "minoritizing logic," in which Eribon attempts to make a claim for considering gays as a legitimate minority whose concerns demand public airing and even restitution. As such, his book is both, in Eribon's words, "a political gesture" and "sometimes deliberately pedagogical in nature."[8] It is clear that his book is meant both for an academic audience and a larger public, one that he hopes to educate about the condition, experience, and lives of gay people—as well as to comfort those queers reading it. Eribon hopes, perhaps, that curious straights with an intellectual bent will read the book and understand better the lives of their gay brothers and sisters.

At the same time, there are passages in *Insult* that suggest that imagining queerness, if one is not already queer, is something of an impossibility. If you haven't been cut in this particular way, you won't know its pain. Eribon asks, "How can the intensity of this shame be understood by those who have never experienced it? How can they understand the strength of the motivations produced by the desire to escape from it?"[9]

The desire to escape from it. *The desire to escape from it.*

I read these words and see myself. I, for so long, wanted to escape from my life, my damaged life. At the same time, though, approaching my late fifties, while I see myself in these words, I also *no longer*

8 Ibid., xvii, 82–86.

9 Ibid., 29.

recognize myself in them. I have ceased to desire *escape*. Don't get me wrong. I would escape if I could, and I see my eventual death as an escape. But desire? No, I don't *desire* it.

I don't *desire* escape.

But I am living with it. I live with the intensity of shame, the damage, the cut. I live with them. Just as I live with the pleasure, the joy, the daring, the defiance. I live with all of it. All of it, all of the time, at the same time. I live with the intensity.

The intensity.

I'm almost done. I can feel it.

The intensity of writing all of these words, assembling these bits and pieces, reflecting on these photographs, this artwork—and then how they are reflecting me, somewhat, somehow, in some way that I reflect back now to you.

Can you see that reflection? Do you recognize part of yourself in it, maybe as you catch just a glimpse of yourself, of who you are, maybe even of who you would like to be—or whom you're running from, whom you're trying to escape?

What cuts do you carry? What cuts on your back, or your arms, or your face—what cuts do you carry with you into the places of joy you seek?

They are there, aren't they?

They are there, and they are so particular, so very particular. I wouldn't rob you of them, even though I wish you healing. And joy. And joy beyond any healing, because I'm not sure I even believe in healing any more.

Once, when asked if my writing helped "heal" me of my damage, my past trauma, the abuse I suffered, I said without missing a beat, "I'll be healed when I'm dead."

I still believe that, even though I do not wish for death. Not anymore. At least not all the time.

No, I wouldn't take your particular cuts away from you. And I don't think Opie would do that either. But it's worth noting that we don't know her pain, not exactly. In the two pictures I've discussed here we don't see her face—a face that would particularize the pain as hers. By not showing her face she's telling us that we cannot know *her particular cut*, her particular pain, even as we see the wounds on her back, on her flesh.

Maybe, you might think, she's hiding her face *from shame*. That is, hiding it *because* she is ashamed and hiding it *from* shame because of what she's done to her body, what she's now, perhaps defiantly, offering us to witness. I'm not sure. Shame is tricky. I'd like to think instead that what she's doing is offering a part of herself that might allow us to see part of *ourselves* in her. Not her face, not the particularity of her, but the broad expanse of back on which we might identify, just a little bit, a fellow traveler, someone who has experienced pain, and damage, and who also pursues pleasure and joy and love.

The art critic Douglas Crimp, in "Mario Montez, For Shame," about a similar set of queer artworks that invite comparable meditations, writes that we can't take on other's identities, but that we can recognize—and possibly share—their vulnerability. He says, "In taking on the shame, I do not share in the other's identity. I simply adopt the other's *vulnerability to being shamed*. In this operation, the other's difference is preserved; it is not claimed as my own. In taking on or taking up his or her shame, I am not attempting to vanquish his or her otherness. I put myself in the place of the other only insofar as I recognize that I too am *prone to shame*."[10]

Yes, yes, that seems right. I, you, we don't "identify." But we see our vulnerability. We share, always, the possibility of vulnerability.

I write about Guibert, Morrisroe, dead of AIDS. I do not know that experience, their experience, but I am prone to the hostility of a culture that sees AIDS as a gay plague. I cannot know the specific suffering of Laura Aguilar, but I am prone to the insults of being overweight and the complex, difficult pleasure of learning to love my large body. I cannot know the racism experienced by Carlos Martiel, coming on the heels of centuries of racialized hate and subjugation, but I can experience my own particular vulnerability to being shamed, to being wounded, to being cut as a queer person. I cannot know

10 Douglas Crimp, "Maria Montez, for Shame," in *"Our Kind of Movie": The Films of Andy Warhol* (Cambridge, MA: MIT Press, 2012), 34, emphasis added.

what it's like to be Catherine Opie, but I see her like a sister, a fellow traveler, and hope she doesn't take that as an insult.

I want to touch the scars on her back—touch in recognition, touch in shared vulnerability, touch even in admiration. Admiration for a life lived queerly, cuts and all.

Cuts and all.

The Aftermath

The first episode of the first season of HBO's *Generation*, about a group of sexually and racially diverse SoCal youth, is all about the phone, the image, the photograph. The very first thing we see in this episode, an establishing image as it were, is a young woman in a mall using her smart phone as a compact, adjusting her makeup, while her friend moans in the bathroom, about to give birth; neither young woman had known that the girl in the bathroom is pregnant.

"Can you Google how to give birth?" the friend screams from behind the closed bathroom door.

The scene shifts to three months earlier, and we see Chester, parading around his high school in a tank top and being duly sent to his guidance counselor, Sam, to discuss this dress code violation. Chester is stunned by how attractive Sam is, commencing a flirtation that we as viewers know is the first salvo of one the series' dramatic arcs. Part of that dramatic salvo hinges on a photograph. Chester points out a picture that Sam has hung up on his wall, a picture of a younger Sam in Japan. Sam tells Chester that the picture was taken when he was the loneliest he's ever been, and he's hung it up on his office wall to remind him that he's never been quite that alone since. The picture, we see as Chester peers at it, is of Sam looking out the window of a tall building.

Another scene, and we see Chester ogling Sam as the counselor stretches on a playing field, preparing for a run, and then Chester heads with a friend to the top of a building overlooking the city skyline at dusk. He takes a selfie of himself sitting on the ledge and then sends it to Sam, saying, "This is what lonely looks like."

Chester heads to a house party to meet up with a secret admirer, but his good time is interrupted when Sam calls him, thinking that Chester's pic is a cry for help. Chester says that no, it's not, it's not a cry for help, that he and a friend were just "rooftopping," but Sam still demands to meet with Chester on Monday to talk. Sam says, "You said this is what loneliness looks like."

Chester responds, "It's fucking beautiful."

Chester then meets his admirer, Nathan, who says he is having the worst night of his life and demands immediately to take a selfie. Chester leans in and encourages Nathan: "It only goes up. And you should get a picture, to remember it'll never be that bad again."

I could go on, but this is enough. The ubiquity of phones is not what's surprising in this episode, the first in a series about SoCal youth, typically wedded to their devices. What draws me in is the *particularity* of the images shown, specifically the photographs — especially the one in Sam's office, then one that Chester takes and sends to Sam in a failed attempt to create connection.[1]

See? I'm like you. I like *you.*

The opening image of a young woman adjusting her makeup with her camera's phone, all too plainly signaling the use of the digitally reflected image of the self to enhance or alter one's performance of self, gives way to a photographic exchange that tries to exceed that self-referentiality and make connection, even if it fails to do so—at least immediately.

But more, so much more. Sam's image and then Chester's image are about what loneliness looks like. Both are queer, so we're tempted—invited—to read the images as ones of *queer loneliness.* They are

1 It's worth noting that Chester wants to connect with Sam through an image of loneliness, but Sam, the counselor, the representative of panoptical psychologizing, reads the image Chester sends not as one of holding pain and possibility together, but only as one of damage that needs addressing, that needs attention, that needs to be depathologized. Chester's image and Sam's response remind us that we cannot control the images we send out into the world. But it's the attempt I am valuing, honoring, and loving here.

images, reminders even, of pain, of the history (in Sam's case) of pain encountered, damage sustained, lingering, remembered.

"It's so fucking beautiful," Chester says.

This is the meeting point—pain and beauty, damage and even the potential for pleasure—that I want to hold in my hand, even as I can't, even as both slip away, like so many digital images, taken, lost, then circulating, resurfacing when you least expect them. Pain and beauty. Damage and pleasure.

Damage. And pleasure.

I'm home alone one afternoon and decide to have some playtime. I am a prodigious masturbator, or at least I have been, before my body's testosterone started to lower with age and I have come to think of pleasuring myself less and less. But I have, for sure, been an ardent self-lover, so much so that I have sometimes wondered if my primary sexual orientation is toward solo sex. By some mythical accounts I should have long ago gone blind. I am, in fact, partially blind due to a stroke, and I can't help but wonder if there's a connection. The mythic strands of puritanical belief hold me tightly, still, after all these years.

Unsurprising that some of my self-love sessions involve bondage, tying myself up in various contorted poses, struggling against my self-imposed bonds. Are there metaphors here? Metonymies of desire, stretching from the cuffs and ropes holding me tight to the homophobic, sexphobic discourses of a culture that has tried to kill me, that wishes I'd never been born in the first place? Too simple, still, to say that I "learn to love the bonds," make erotic play out of the punishment directed at me? I'm reminded of Deleuze on masochism: "The masochistic ego is only apparently crushed by the superego. What insolence and humor, what irrepressible defiance and ultimate triumph lie hidden behind an ego that claims to be so weak." Sure, I guess, but this is so . . . vitalist, so making the pervert speak toward a Spinozian ecstasy. Part of me loves that my kink is the fodder of high theory. Part of me is not so sure I buy it.

Like today, I head to my basement with a time-lock, an ingenious device, a tube filled with frozen water (I'd put it in the freezer the night before) with two metal cuffs attached at either end, a self-bondage toy that, once you lock yourself into it, traps you until enough ice melts to free the cuffs. I plan to lock myself up with my hands suspended over my head, the time-lock attached to a pipe in the basement. But not just this. I give myself a couple of suppositories, put on a large adult diaper, attach a leg-spreader to keep my feet apart, and then, only then, do I lock my hands into the suspended time-lock cuffs, stretching my body vertically taut.

Disclaimer: I am not an infantilist or even a diaper fetishist. But like many kinksters, especially those who like to play alone, I like the idea of (nearly) inescapable bondage, tying myself up in torturous ways and struggling against the bonds. The suppositories and diapers, I admit, come from stuff I've seen online, something to add to the predicament—some folks literally call this kind of thing "predicament bondage," a test, a self-administered test, the need to struggle and try to escape before something awful happens: in this case, uncontrollably shitting yourself. You may not believe me, but I'll tell you plainly: I do not want to shit myself. I'm not into shit or even piss for that matter. While I've felt my own piss stream's warmth, I do not want to piss on or be pissed on, much less shit on or be shat on. I'm interested in the predicament. Ok, maybe possibly also the humiliation of coming close to shitting myself. Possibly.

But I'm not prepared, I'm not prepared for this. The suppositories work a lot faster than I had anticipated. My body stretched, my legs spread, my gut starts to spasm almost as soon as I cuff my hands. Within minutes, I'm clenching my anus, clench clench, but it's too late and I'm soon filling my diaper, shitting myself, uncontrollably shitting myself. I'm regretting that I opted for more than just one suppository. I wanted to challenge myself . . . and I lost. And now I'm stuck here, a diaper full of shit, a grown-ass man with a diaper full of shit, stuck until enough ice melts for me to wriggle my cuffed hands out of the time-lock and waddle to the bathroom to clean myself up.

I am more than humiliated. I can barely describe the welter of emotions, the hot shame of it all. I couldn't control my own body but, even more, I put myself in a position, willingly, to experience this. No, it's not scarring my back like Catherine Opie, or cuffing myself naked for gawking crowds in the Guggenheim like Carlos Martiel. It's not draping myself across desert rocks and photographing myself like Laura Aguilar, a fat spectacle of self. And it's certainly not the pain of AIDS like Mark Morrisroe and Hervé Guibert felt them, probably shitting themselves, shitting themselves, shitting out their flesh until there's nothing left—and then daring to record it for others to see. No, this is not any of that, even if part of me imagines that it is, wants it to be, just a little bit, just a little bit of shared suffering, just a little bit of shared recognition of vulnerability, of shame.

But it's not.

Instead, this feels somehow beyond damage even as, intellectually, just hanging there having soiled myself on purpose, I know it's not, not beyond anything. It is. It just is, and I'll hang here until I am free. It's not erotic, not really. I am not hard. I am not aroused. It is not, à la Deleuze, irrepressible defiance and ultimate triumph. It is, rather . . . intense.

Intense.

I hang in my diaper for about an hour. The ice melts, the cuffs release me. I stagger upstairs, soiled, to clean myself off. To clean myself off.

And I wonder, will I ever, ever, fully clean myself off? And what if I don't? What then?

And I wonder, does it even, does it ever matter if I'm never fully clean?

I wonder.

Then I shower, and rest, and put away my toys, the cuffs, the diapers, put the towels in the hamper. I wonder, and rest.

Until next time.

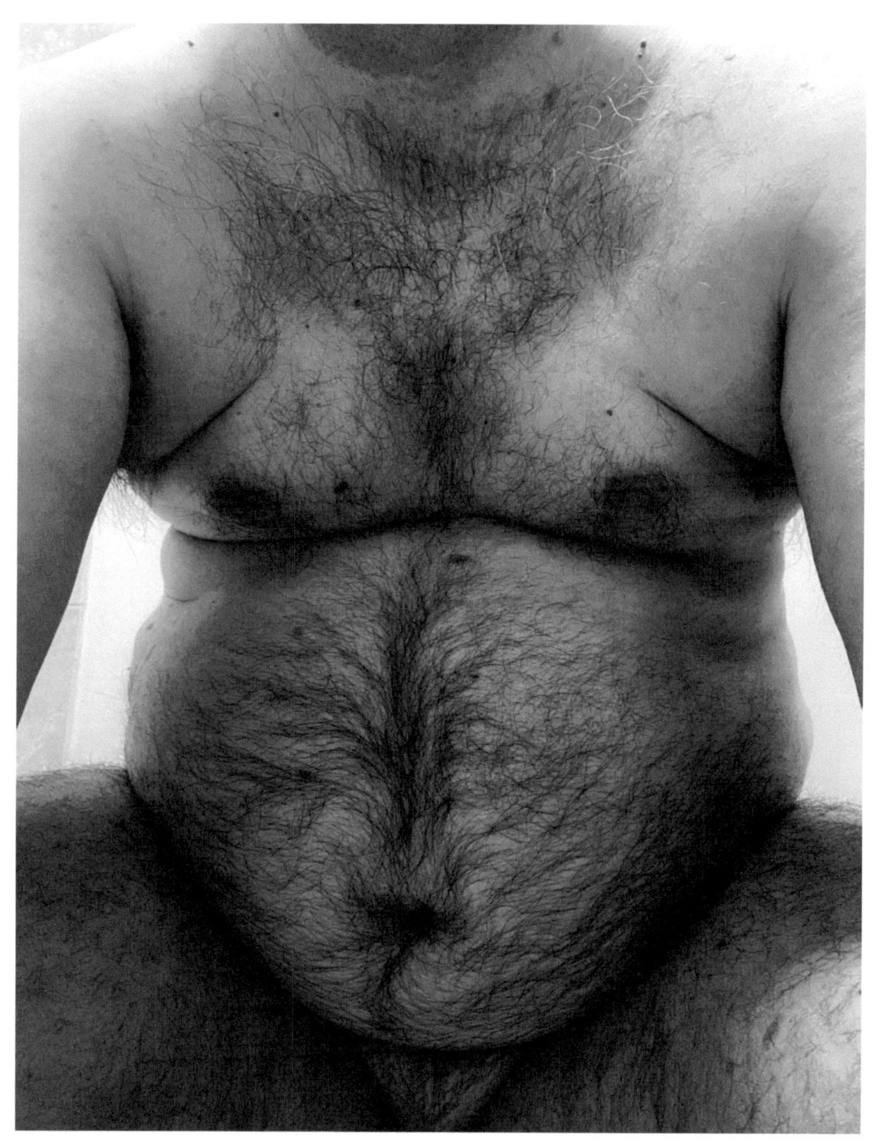

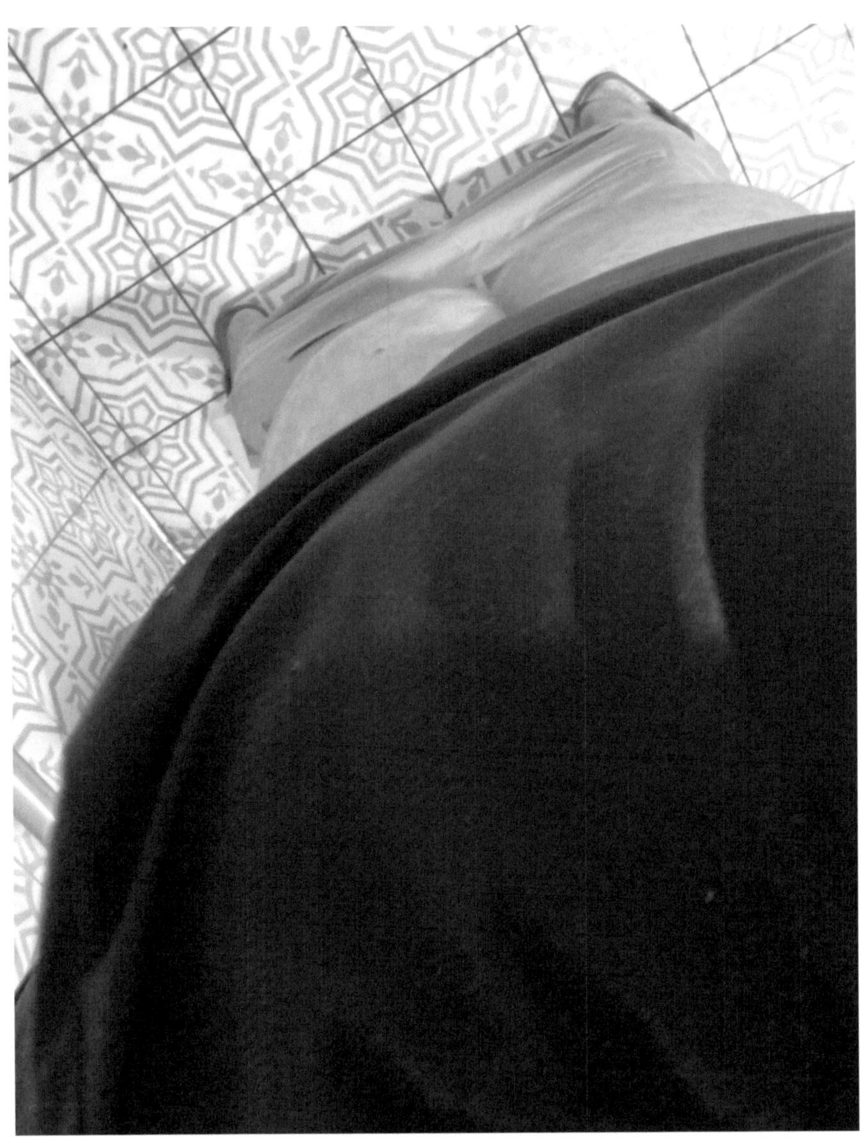

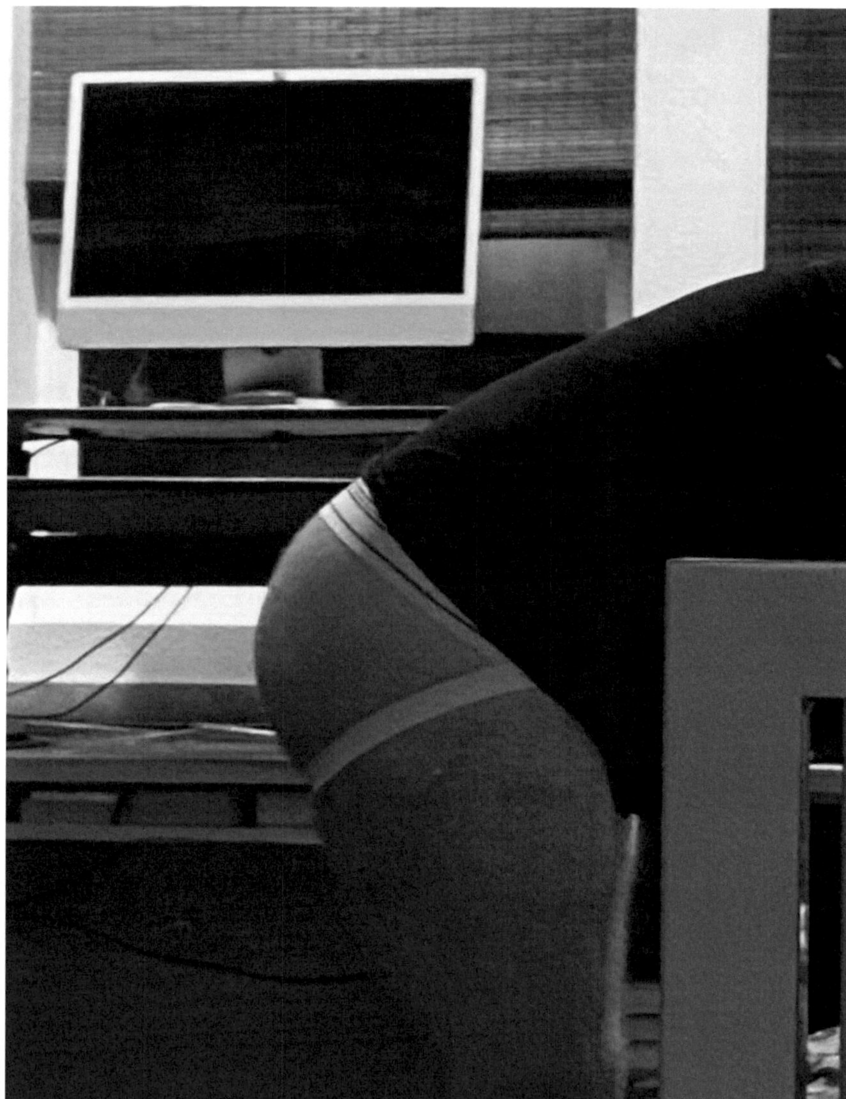

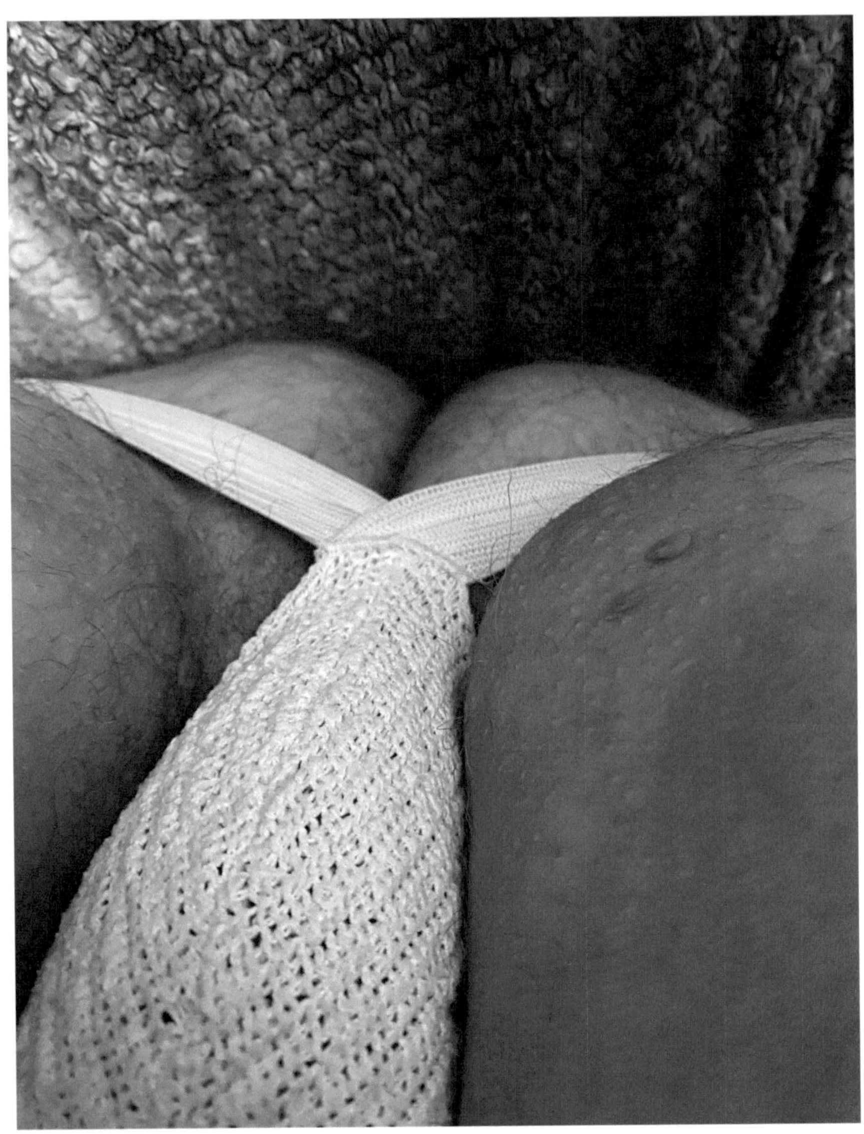

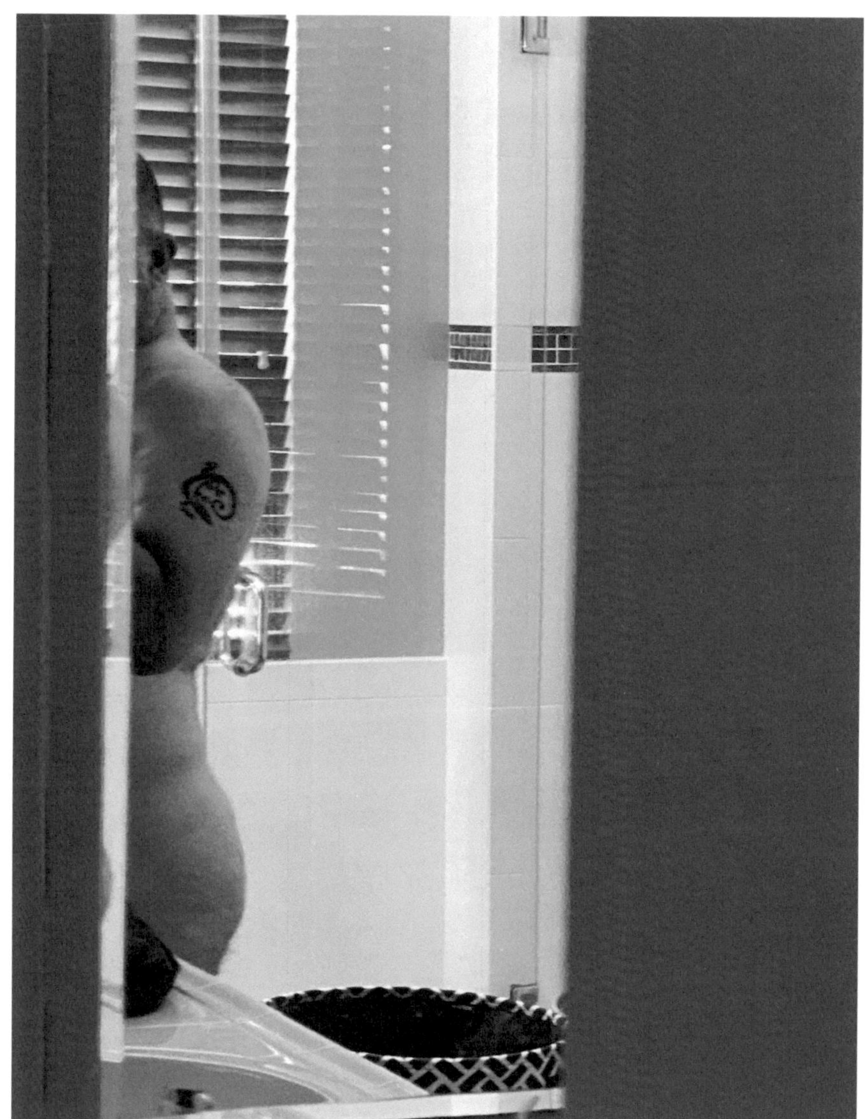

Acknowledgments

I've written a few acknowledgments in my time, and I always know that I'm doing them wrong. Someone will be left out (usually more than one someone), and someone else is likely to feel overthanked for a book that they might not necessarily want to be associated with (and this feels like one of those books). But I do the best I can, however damaged the result might be.

First and foremost, Fred Nachbaur and the team at Fordham University Press are among the finest professionals with whom I've ever had the pleasure of working. I'm so grateful to Fordham for providing a home for this book. Thanks as well to my external reviewers who provided me thoughts and insights that have immeasurably made this book better than it was when I first submitted it.

I've been fortunate to have many interlocutors and fellow travelers along the way while writing this book, including the following (in no particular order) who have helped me not only think about damage conceptually but who have also been patient with my own many damages: Karen Yescavage, Jacqueline Rhodes, Sherryl Vint, David Wallace, James Kyung-Jin Lee, Christian Haines, Catherine Malabou, Scott Branson, Julia Lupton, Bridget Cooks, elin o'Hara slavick, Susan C. Jarratt, Rebekah Sheldon, Michelle Latiolais, Jami Bartlett, Alexander Catchings, Nasrin Rahimieh, George Lang, Paweł Frelik, Antoinette LaFarge, Juli Carson, Eileen Joy, Paul Walker, Amy Robillard, Katherine Mack, and Paul J. Willis.

Of these folks, some special notes: Jackie kindly invited me to give a talk at the University of Texas at Austin, where I presented some early work on this project, and Christian published some of my thoughts on Mark Morrisroe in the *Journal of Utopian Studies*. I'm grateful for their kind interlocution and furtherance of my thoughts. A symposium I hosted at UC Irvine on “Anarchy, Plasticity, Worldbuilding” was also instrumental in helping me theorize concepts related to damage; Catherine and Scott were wonderful thought partners. Rebekah and I hosted an online symposium during COVID on “Queer Utopias,” and that project sparked my thinking on the damages that inevitably must be worked through (and never forgotten) en route to any utopian dreaming. Katherine Mack and I hosted and led a Rhetoric Society of America Summer Institute session on memoir, and I learned so much from our participants—and especially Katherine—on life writing that has found its way into these pages. Paul Walker kindly published some of my thinking on fatness in *Intraspection*, and I am still grateful for having had that opportunity. And Paul J. Willis, founder and director of the annual Saints and Sinners LGBTQ Literary Festival, has been such a welcoming and generous force in providing me a regular platform in New Orleans for sharing ideas, thoughts, and writing. With gratitude to you all—and to those I am inevitably forgetting. Apologies, and gratitude.

For assistance with photography permissions, much thanks to Christopher Velasco, Christine Guibert, Catherine Opie and the folks at Regen projects, Carlos Martiel and his staff, and the folks at P.P.O.W. and Fotomuseum Winterthur.

Finally, without doubt, Mack McCoy is more than a husband; he is the one around and through and with whom I build my world on this planet, both despite and in light of the damages we bring to that project. I can’t imagine building a world with anyone else, however damaged I make it through my own ineptitude. Much love, always, dear boo.

Jonathan Alexander is Chancellor's Professor of English and Gender & Sexuality Studies at UC Irvine. Author of more than twenty books, he blends memoir and criticism in work often described as autotheory. His titles include *Writing & Desire*, *Stroke Book* (Fordham), and a trilogy—*Creep: A Life, a Theory, an Apology*; *Bullied: The Story of an Abuse*; and *Dear Queer Self*. Honors include a Lambda Literary finalist nod, a gold IPPY, an INDIES finalist citation, and the Lavender Rhetorics Award.